IN LEAPS AND BOUNDS

IN LEAPS AND BOUNDS
Psychic Development and its Facilitation in Treatment

Salman Akhtar

PHOENIX
PUBLISHING HOUSE
firing the mind

First published in 2022 by
Phoenix Publishing House Ltd
62 Bucknell Road
Bicester
Oxfordshire OX26 2DS

Chapter 2 is reprinted, with permission, from *Growing Up: Revisiting Child Development Theories and Their Application to Patients of All Ages*. eds. H. Parens and S. Akhtar, pp. 1–38, Lanham, MD: Lexington Books.

British Library Cataloguing in Publication Data

A C.I.P. for this book is available from the British Library

ISBN-13: 978-1-912691-91-3

Typeset by Medlar Publishing Solutions Pvt Ltd, India

www.firingthemind.com

To

ROHAN & SHALINI MAITRA

whose development I have watched with tenderness and care

Contents

Acknowledgments

Though not formally trained as a child psychoanalyst, I have greatly benefited from my contacts with specialists in this field. Setting aside the momentary encounters with Anna Freud and Margaret Mahler during which I mumbled something inane, though reverential, and they indulgently nodded their heads, it was the long-term supervision I had with the renowned child analyst (the late) Dr. Selma Kramer that gave an indelible developmental stance to my clinical work with adults.

Among other child psychoanalysts who taught me during my candidacy at the Philadelphia Psychoanalytic Institute (1979–1986) were (the late) Drs. Alexis Burland, LeRoy Byerley, and Joseph Rudolph, as well as Drs. Newell and Ruth Fischer, James Goldstein, and Henri Parens. My postgraduate contact with Drs. Jennifer Bonovitz, Hossein Etezady, Theodore Fallon, Corrine Masur, Barbara Shapiro, William Singletary, Ann Smolen, and Barbara Young also proved to be instructive.

I was fortunate to receive kind attention from many distinguished child analysts outside of Philadelphia, especially (the late) Drs. Helen Meyers and Bernard Pacella, and Drs. Anni Bergman, Harold Blum, and Fred Pine. More recently, other outstanding child analysts have generously responded to my requests for consultation and academic help.

These include Jaswant Guzder, Christine Kieffer, Mali Mann, James Herzog, Leon Hoffman, Kerry Kelly Novick, Jack Novick, and Kathryn Zerbe.

In the realm of adult development, I learnt much from personally interacting with (the late) Drs. Stanley Cath, Ruth Lax, Robert Prall, and Leo Madow as well as Drs. Calvin Colarusso and John Munder Ross.

Dr. Rajnish Mago and Ms. Ray-Ling Hou found many important citations from literature for me, Dr. Nathaniel Graham provided me a clinical vignette included in this book, and my assistant Ms. Jan Wright prepared the manuscript of this book with her usual grace and diligence. Ms. Kelsey Leon helped not only by some last-minute typing, but far more importantly, by providing meaningful assistance during the copy editing process of the manuscript.

I thank all these individuals. I am also grateful to my patients, my personal friends, my children, and my ever supportive life partner Muge. Without them, the work I am offering you here would not have been possible.

About the author

Salman Akhtar, MD, is professor of psychiatry at Jefferson Medical College and a training and supervising analyst at the Psychoanalytic Center of Philadelphia. He has served on the editorial boards of the *International Journal of Psychoanalysis*, the *Journal of the American Psychoanalytic Association*, and the *Psychoanalytic Quarterly*. His more than 400 publications include 103 books, of which the following 21 are solo-authored: *Broken Structures* (1992), *Quest for Answers* (1995), *Inner Torment* (1999), *Immigration and Identity* (1999), *New Clinical Realms* (2003), *Objects of Our Desire* (2005), *Regarding Others* (2007), *Turning Points in Dynamic Psychotherapy* (2009), *The Damaged Core* (2009), *Comprehensive Dictionary of Psychoanalysis* (2009), *Immigration and Acculturation* (2011), *Matters of Life and Death* (2011), *The Book of Emotions* (2012), *Psychoanalytic Listening* (2013), *Good Stuff* (2013), *Sources of Suffering* (2014), *No Holds Barred* (2016), *A Web of Sorrow* (2017), *Mind, Culture, and Global Unrest* (2018), *Silent Virtues* (2019), and *Tales of Transformation* (2022).

Dr. Akhtar has delivered many prestigious invited lectures including a plenary address at the 2nd International Congress of the International Society for the Study of Personality Disorders in Oslo, Norway (1991), an invited plenary paper at the 2nd International Margaret S. Mahler Symposium in Cologne, Germany (1993), an invited plenary paper at the Rencontre Franco-Americaine de Psychanalyse meeting in Paris, France (1994), a keynote address at the 43rd IPA Congress in Rio de Janeiro, Brazil (2005), the plenary address at the 150th Freud Birthday Celebration sponsored by the Dutch Psychoanalytic Society and the Embassy of Austria in Leiden, Holland (2006), the inaugural address at the first IPA-Asia Congress in Beijing, China (2010), and the plenary address at the Fall Meetings of the American Psychoanalytic Association in 2017.

Dr. Akhtar is the recipient of numerous awards including the American Psychoanalytic Association's Edith Sabshin Award (2000), Columbia University's Robert Liebert Award for Distinguished Contributions to Applied Psychoanalysis (2004), the American Psychiatric Association's Kun Po Soo Award (2004) and Irma Bland Award for being the Outstanding Teacher of Psychiatric Residents in the country (2005). He received the highly prestigious Sigourney Award (2012) for distinguished contributions to psychoanalysis. In 2013, he gave the commencement address at graduation ceremonies of the Smith College School of Social Work in Northampton, MA. Dr. Akhtar's books have been translated into many languages, including German, Italian, Romanian, Serbian, Spanish, and Turkish. A true Renaissance man, Dr. Akhtar has served as the film review editor for the *International Journal of Psychoanalysis*, and is currently serving as the book review editor for the *International Journal of Applied Psychoanalytic Studies*. He has published fifteen collections of poetry and serves as a scholar-in-residence at the Inter-Act Theatre Company in Philadelphia.

Introduction

This book consists of three essays on psychoanalytic understanding of personality development and the utilization of such understanding in treating patients. *The first essay* covers the period from the earliest infancy through childhood to the adolescent turmoil and its resolution. It addresses the following developmental landmarks:

- Renouncing omnipotence and accepting reality
- Establishing a satisfactory bond with the mother
- Moving toward autonomy and independence
- Benefiting from contact with the father and the attendant triangulation
- Increasing cognitive sophistication
- Acquiring a moral sense
- Consolidating identity and the capacity for romantic love.

The second essay deals with the period after adolescence and addresses the psychosocial challenges characteristic of young adulthood, midlife, and old age. It elucidates the following major milestones:

- Consolidating a life dream, finding a mentor, and establishing a work identity
- Assuming the role of a wage-earner and "house-holder"
- Enjoying sex, love, and marriage
- Becoming a parent and partaking of the attendant pleasures and responsibilities
- Noticing and accepting changes in one's body and their impact upon identity
- Encountering limits in diverse psychosocial realms
- Accommodating changes in one's relationship with parents
- Letting go of children and not letting an "empty nest" become an "empty chest"
- Becoming a grandparent
- Downsizing and retiring from one's job
- Dealing with the deaths of friends, siblings, and spouses
- Getting really old, facing infirmities, and preparing to die.

The third essay builds upon the foregoing conceptual discourse *and* deals with the various ways in which the resultant deepened understanding of psychic development can inform our clinical approach. Emphatically reminding the practitioner to keep in mind that development is a lifelong process, this essay provides clear guidelines for facilitating growth by conducting "developmental work" with our patients. Needless to add, such work is an additive to—not a replacement of—our customary methods of listening, affirmation, confrontation, interpretation, and reconstruction. The guidelines offered here include:

- Providing nonverbal ego-strengthening measures
- Creating psychic space for thinking
- Helping the patient find words for inner experiences
- Continuing to work despite what might seem reprehensible in the patient's material
- Remembering that an occasional regression is integral to development
- Validating the patient's reality
- Restraining the greed for interpretation when a thwarted developmental tendency makes its first appearance
- Seeing goodness and potential for growth in the patient

- Enhancing the sense of personal agency in the patient
- Helping the patient talk about issues related to mortality and death.

The complex tapestry woven by these three essays is sandwiched between a *Prologue* and an *Epilogue*. The former defines and describes what I have euphemistically called the "pre-self"; this "structure" refers to the foundations of the self laid down by events occurring before our birth and during our intrauterine life. The latter offers a delineation of the "post-self" which involves our continued existence as memories in the hearts of our loved ones. Acting in unison, the five chapters of this book deepen our understanding of the nuances of human development and of the interventions that we clinicians can make to facilitate its desirable unfolding.

Prologue

CHAPTER ONE

The pre-self

In their seminal monograph *The Psychological Birth of Human Infant*, Mahler, Pine, and Bergman (1975) assert that there is a nearly two-year gap between the child's biological and psychological births. By "biological birth," the authors mean the transition from the prenatal to postnatal period of life. By "psychological birth," they mean the emergence of a stable and coherent personal core which possesses a sense of autonomy and self-agency. Their work, painstakingly elucidating the journey between these two epochs (via the phases of symbiosis and separation–individuation), is well accepted and, at least in the North American psychoanalytic corpus, has become deeply assimilated in the mainstream.

To be sure, this line of thinking has merit, but it is also possible that the ontogenetic traffic might actually be flowing in the opposite direction. In other words, "psychological birth" of the human infant might precede, not follow, his or her "biological birth." It is to this latter proposal that I give the designation the "pre-self". This "proto-psychic" structure refers to the features of our selves that are derived from the factors operative long before we begin our postnatal existence in this world. Such factors are wide-ranging and can hardly be fully addressed in the limited corpus of this prologue. However, this ought not preclude succinct comments on the most important of them.

One, our being born as black or white, poor or rich, as members of a despised minority or a well-protected, even smug, majority, and in a given era of human history and particular region of the globe can affect the "basic core" (Weil, 1970) that will evolve and have a life-altering impact upon such self's direction. A black child born in apartheid-era South Africa of not so long ago absorbed a radically different societal gaze into his or her self-system than a ruling class, white child did. The "mental pain of minorities" (Akhtar, 2014a) is not a static, cross-sectional phenomenon; it trickles downwards in the veins of the subsequent generations. Similarly, being born as a Muslim baby in India is not the same thing as in Pakistan; the former shall remain forever vulnerable to be blamed not only for the 1947 partition of India but for the Muslim plunder of Hindu temples nearly a thousand years ago. More examples can be readily given but the point has been made. Where one is born and under what light or shadow of history makes a difference to the postnatal self one would develop.

Two, the unique genetic combination each of us will receive from the encounter of our mother's ovum and our father's sperm shall, at least in part, determine how we appear as infants and children and what we become as adults. No two children of the same biological parents are exactly alike; even monozygotic twins can show motoric, cognitive, and behavioral differences from the time soon after their birth, differences that might persist in their adulthood (Riese, 1990; Saudino et al., 2000). We, as individuals, have no control as to whether we will get our father's built-in athleticism or our mother's literary talent; it is a coin toss in the end.

Three, it is now well established that a baby is not a tabula rasa. Each baby brings his or her own "temperament" (Thomas & Chess, 1977), that is, affectomotor propensities and an own way of engaging the caretaking environment. The work of psychologically informed infant and child observers (Emde, 1980, 1981; Greenspan, 1980; Lichtenberg, 1982, 1983; and Stern, 1985, to name a few) is of great significance here. Essentially, these investigations demonstrate how the infant's innate capacity for affectivity, attachment, and emotional signaling interact with the caretaker's, especially the mother's, cues and responses and how such "dialogue" (Spitz, 1960) firms up the foundation of the self. The pre-self thus shapes the self.

Four, lingering effects of the intrauterine experience also show up in the postnatal proclivities and preferences of the baby. Ancient myths and folklore are replete with "proofs" of this. Psychoanalysts have speculated about the potential links between the fetal experience and postnatal behavior. Balint (1959), in his later formulation of "ocnophilia" (love of objects) and "philobatism" (love of spaces), correlates the latter to the free-flowing freedom of the fetus and, more recently, Grunberger (1989) traced the origins of its narcissistic "monad" to the carefree and objectless intrauterine life. On a "scientific" and empirical plane, the work of Piontelli (1992) is paramount. She observed eleven fetuses (three singletons and four sets of twins) using ultrasound scans and, after their births, followed them for four years. Carefully recording features of their psychomotor development and treating one of these children in psychoanalytic psychotherapy led Piontelli to draw significant conclusions about the uniqueness of each fetus and the postnatal emergence of authenticity in them. She also witnessed the influence of maternal emotions during pregnancy upon the evolution of the psychological styles of their offspring. All in all, Piontelli found marked behavioral and psychological continuities between prenatal (pre-self in my terminology) and postnatal lives.

Five, the wishful or dreaded fantasies in the minds of our parents and grandparents also lay the blueprint for our postnatal selves. Some children are conceived to salvage a fledgling parental marriage. Some are brought into this world—more so in collective societies where "familial self" (Roland, 1988) is normative—as a gift to the grandparents. Still others are "replacement children" (Poznanski, 1972) whose mothers became pregnant during the course of bereavement and mourning; once born, these babies are prone to be viewed as "special" since their existence is supposed to heal the mother's *Seelenschmerz* (Freud, 1926d) or mental pain. However, they are also viewed as useless since they are not actually the deceased person. Such split messaging bifurcates their selves into grandiose and morose sectors (Volkan & Ast, 1997). And, to wit, the process leading to such outcome has begun long before their birth. The list of parental agendas that propel having a child is inexhaustible, to be sure. The family's need to have a rescuer, a jester, a proud individual, a psychologically dead person, and "the crazy one" is a silent but influential current constituting our pre-selves.

Six, birth order can also have an effect on the self that will subsequently emerge. Alfred Adler (1870–1937), an early pupil and collaborator of Freud, was the first among psychologists to underscore the importance of birth order. He felt that being a firstborn, second born, or the youngest one exerted a significant influence upon the fundamental emotional orientation of the child. Adler states that the firstborn child feels

> Dethroned by the birth of the next sibling … [and] a child who has lost his power, the small kingdom he ruled, understands better than others the importance of power and authority. [The second born, in contrast,] behaves as if he were in a race, is under full steam all the time, and trains continually to surpass his older brother and conquer him. (Cited in Ansbacher and Ansbacher, 1956, 378–379)

Adler proposed that the firstborns are generally power hungry, the second borns rarely able to endure an overseeing authority, and the last borns ("the babies" of the family) late bloomers. In a thorough scrutiny of Adler's ideas and adding his own meticulous and impressive research, Sulloway (1997) questioned such generalizations. He stated:

> Children do not inherit special genes for being firstborns or lastborns, only genes for engaging successfully in competition for parental investment. The family environment determines how these competitive tendencies are expressed in terms of personality, every first born is a potential last born, and vice-versa. The psychological consequences of birth order provide compelling evidence for the formative role of the family environment. (p. xv)

Sulloway places the issue of birth order in the context of gender, temperament, parental attitudes, and what he calls "sibling strategies" (pp. 67–71) or action plans different siblings evolve to obtain as much parental attention and love as they can. While rendering the study of birth order far more nuanced than its original form in Adler's work, Sulloway does acknowledge that,

> Throughout most of childhood, firstborns enjoy the advantage of being bigger, stronger, and smarter than their younger siblings. The possession of these attributes makes it natural for the first born to feel more self-assured than lastborns ... Among later borns, lesser physical size suggests strategies that minimize physical confrontations. Prudent later born strategies include acquiescing to first born demands, cooperating, pleasing, whining, and appealing to parents for protection ... Relative to firstborns, later borns are also reported to be more altruistic, empathetic, and peer oriented. (pp. 68–69)

Seven, the presence or absence of inborn talents and congenital anomalies are also attributes of our pre-selves. It is well established that those born with remarkable talents (e.g., singing, drawing, mathematical skills) do well not only during their childhood but in adult life as well. This "advantage" often survives adverse environmental conditions (e.g., poverty, unstable home) and might even contribute to the person's characterological "resilience" (Hauser et al., 2006; Parens et al., 2008) and "grit" (Duckworth, 2016). On the other hand, congenital defects (e.g., cleft palate, club foot, facial deformity) and tragic occurrences before one's birth (e.g., father's death while the mother was pregnant) leave indelible marks on the self that later evolves. Freud's (1916d) concept of "exceptions" addresses this very point. Elsewhere I have distilled the essential components of his proposal:

> Individuals who fall under this rubric display four characteristics: (i) as children they suffered from some illness or mishap which imposed "an unjust disadvantage" (Freud, 1916d, p. 313) upon them, (ii) they did not contribute to the occurrence of this problem and were truly guiltless, (iii) due to such unearned suffering they feel desiring to be spared of any further demand in life and are especially abhorrent to rules and regulation, and (iv) their feeling of being an "exception" often entitles them to immoral or illegal behavior. (Akhtar, 2009a, p. 99)

In contradictory ways, predetermined talents and randomly inflected misfortunes both prepare the groundwork (pre-self) for the later self to emerge. Here the way the family, especially the mother, welcomes her newborn and treats him or her during childhood plays a profound formative role.

Eight, the human infant is born weak, helpless, and dependent upon others for survival. Winnicott's oft-cited aphorism of 1940 that "there is no such thing as an infant" (1960a, p. 39) aptly describes this situation; a baby exists in the context of the mother–baby dyad. The look in the mother's eyes (Wright, 1991), breastfeeding, exposure to mother's skin color (McDonald, 1970), availability of her overall body for nourishment and haven (Pruett, 1988), and her capacity to absorb hostile attacks by her infant (Klein, 1935; Mahler et al., 1975; Winnicott, 1960a) and remain available as a "secure base" (Bowlby, 1960) are among the myriad factors giving shape, color, and direction to the baby's future self. Clearly, all this depends upon the mother's own well-being, especially the sense of security within the family and her intrinsic mental health. There has accrued a vast body of literature (Allison & Furstenberg, 1989; Amato et al., 1994; Musick & Meier, 2010) that suggests that the mother's mental health is one of the most significant, if not the most significant, determinant of a child's mental health. An important point to remember here though is that the mother's mental health (or psychopathology) may be her own trait or may emanate from the overall familial context.

Finally, the overall integrity of the family and home exerts a profound impact upon how the child is received and raised. Families in constant discord, scarce caretaking resources, endemic unhappiness, marked social isolation, and warring parents are vulnerable to bringing an "unwelcome child" (Ferenczi, 1929) into this world and thus cause permanent damage to his or her core self representation. The auxiliary role of grandparents, uncles and aunts, and even non-familial figures (e.g., nannies, school teachers, clergy, high school athletic coaches) come into play and can exact considerable ameliorative influence in the child's environment (Akhtar, 2005a).

To sum up, it is clear that a large number of factors that are present (or absent) *before* a child's actual arrival in this world make up a welcome mat for him or her. This is what I have termed pre-self here. The significance of such formulation to the conduct of psychotherapy and psychoanalysis is two-fold: (i) the analyst has to validate the role such factors might have played in a patient's difficulties and help the patient mourn their occurrence and deepen his or her knowledge of how these factors have altered the patient's life; (ii) the analyst should permit himself or herself to go beyond Freud who considered the intrauterine experience of the child to be a matter of "retrospective phantasizing" (1918b, p. 103), and keep the possibility open for considering that the fetal existence might leave dim residues that are unremarkable but play a silent, baseline role in one's preferences for closed versus open spaces (Balint, 1959), one's sleeping postures and one's overall proprioceptive sensibilities (Piontelli, 1987, 1988). The analyst might want to familiarize himself or herself with Philip Ployé's (2006)[1] observation that some patients

> relate to the therapist as if they—or at least points of themselves—were reliving and re-enacting a foetal level of relatedness … and [in such cases] … the countertransference, too, can sometimes be seen to operate at a pre- or perinatal level—that is, the therapist can either experience, or even act out in his or her countertransference, the reactions that the patient's mother may have gone through—and may later be revealed as having actually gone through—during her pregnancy or labor. (pp. 2–3; italics in the original)

This pre-self thing is thus a bit mysterious and elusive at its base but that ought not preclude our seriously considering it and seeing its psychic shadows, echoes, and reverberations in the postnatal self that comes into being at the time of our birth and becomes our tour guide through the complex, meandering, and yet exhilaratingly meaningful journey of life.

[1] Ployé (2006) reminds us that the term "foetal transference" was used for the first time by Symington (1981, p. 195).

Part I

Conceptual basis

CHAPTER TWO

From birth and infancy through childhood to the end of adolescence

Fall of 1996. It has been almost a decade since I completed my psychoanalytic training. And, for the past six years, I have been helping my esteemed supervisor, Selma Kramer (1920–2000), organize our psychoanalytic society's annual symposium held in honor of the renowned child analyst, Margaret Mahler (1897–1985). Though fifty years old, I am regarded as a young analyst. I am excited about my field, brimming with ideas, and have published a few fairly decent papers.

One day, a letter arrives in the mail. It is written by the well-known New York-based child analyst, Helen Meyers (1925–2010). Representing the program committee of the IPA (International Psychoanalytical Association) Congress next year in Barcelona, she is inviting me to present a child analytic case in detail at that meeting in Spain. I am thrilled. The heart of my ambitious self is beating hard. I have visions of a spellbound audience, taking in every word I utter, absorbing every deft movement of my thought. I have them mesmerized. There is only one problem, though: I am not a child analyst, have never treated a child even in psychotherapy. In other words, I have no clinical experience to offer, nothing to present. But, my desire for fame and success wants to disregard this reality, begs me to make something up, pretend to be a child analyst, and not give up this alluring opportunity. Thankfully, my ethical and rational self wins the day. I call Dr. Meyers on the phone and explain my handicap. I am relieved. My superego is at rest. She, however, seems unhappy and deeply puzzled. She says: "You're not a child analyst?!", in a voice dripping with disbelief. Before I can say anything, she adds, "Then, why are you always hanging out with child analysts?" I have no answer to this question and mumble something inane back.

Later, a search for the answer to her question leads me to deeper self-reflection, more self-analysis, and further knowledge of my own childhood. But, that is not what I am offering here today. What I am presenting is an overall summary of what I've gathered by reading and "hanging out with child analysts" about child development. I hope to highlight areas where consensus prevails and areas where unresolved questions exist. I explicate the former in the hope of demonstrating the solidity of our ontogenetic formulations. I elucidate the latter with the aim of stimulating further exploration and bridge-building. Before delving into these matters, however, let me enter some caveats.

Some caveats

First, I am not a child analyst and my scholarship of this realm is not exhaustive. This is especially true of more recent child observational studies which I have not kept up with, as the knowledgeable eye shall readily notice. For this shortcoming, I apologize not only to the reader but to those investigators whose work I have failed to include here.

Second, the cisgender and heteronormative bent of this discourse is reflective of my limited knowledge of the newly emergent psychoanalytic literature on LGBT issues and not due to theoretical bias. Wherever possible, I have added corrective notes and footnotes to address these issues though it may not be enough for everyone as "compensation" for this particular weakness of my contribution.

Third, the developmental scheme delineated in this contribution pertains to children raised in an "average expectable environment" (Hartmann, 1939). It might not apply to children who are highly vulnerable (Cohen et al., 1993, 1995, 1999), invulnerable (Anthony &

Cohler, 1987), orphaned at a young age (Akhtar, 2011b; Furman, 1974), or raised in highly traumatizing circumstances (Smolen, 2013, 2016).

Fourth, the material gathered here comes from considerably diverse sources and this renders me vulnerable to being accused of mixing the proverbial apples with oranges. It might be questioned whether data from child observational studies, clinical treatment of children, reconstructions during adult analyses, and experience-distant theory building can be so seamlessly integrated as I have attempted to do here.

Finally, despite casting my net wide, I have not been able to include important insights regarding child development from the fields of neonatology and pediatrics, social anthropology, gender studies, ethology, neurophysiology, and modern genetics. My oeuvre is largely restricted to psychoanalysis though I have included some pioneering contributions from the neighboring field of general psychology as well.

Having outlined these limitations of my reach, let me now proceed to describing those areas of child development where a reasonable consensus among various scholars prevails.

Areas of agreement

As far as normal child development goes, most psychoanalysts agree upon the following proposals: (i) chronological growth of the child is accompanied by an increasing renunciation of infantile omnipotence and the sense of entitlement that comes with it, (ii) secure bonding with early caregivers, especially the mother, constitutes the bedrock of ego development, (iii) it takes considerable time after birth for a coherent psychological self to emerge and a well-sustained sense of separateness and autonomy to be established; these are the fundamental structures necessary for genuine attachment and genuine separation reactions,[2] (iv) the child's father also plays an important role in his or her emotional

---

[2] "Genuine attachment" to others in adult life is characterized by (i) actual knowledge of the love object, (ii) some scope for ambivalence, and (iii) understanding and accepting the separateness of the other's mind. "Genuine separation reaction" is characterized by "low-keyedness" (Mahler et al., 1975) and mournful longing. Reactions to separation with despair, disorientation and incoherence, suicidal thoughts, murderous rage, or promiscuous replacement of the love object are different; they betray "separateness anxiety" (Pine, 1979) and not "separation anxiety."

growth, (v) cognitive sophistication accrues over time and results in the replacement of egocentric perception and magical thinking by logically governed and temporally anchored thought, (vi) a sense of morality (including concern for others) gradually evolves, and (vii) consolidation of identity and of the capacity for romantic love occurs during adolescence. Let me now explicate these seven issues in brief subsections.

Renouncing omnipotence and accepting reality

There is widespread consensus among child psychoanalysts and neonatal researchers that the sense of reality (including reality awareness, reality testing, and reality acceptance) dawns upon the child only gradually. Neurophysiological maturation facilitates this development but experiential factors also play an important role here. Three such factors include (i) the difference between the visual reach and the tactile reach of the neonate, (ii) the rhythms and events of nature, including the alternation of days and nights, and (iii) the fact that while the child can automatically release certain of his (taken to mean any child) tensions, he is dependent upon his caregivers for the release of certain other tensions.

The first factor (the difference between the neonate's visual and tactile reach) teaches the young one that the objects in the world, even though visible to him, are out of his physical reach. This implies that he is small, has limited powers, and is not omnipotent. It also tells him that there is an entire world out there that is not merged with him, not under his control. The second factor (the events and rhythms of nature) is similarly instructive. The child has little to say about whether the day fades into night or the night evolves into day, whether it rains or whether there is a clap of thunder, a blinding moment of lightning, and so on. Nature, imperious in its own ways, punctures infantile omnipotence.[3] Finally, and most importantly, it is the "peremptory demands of internal needs" (Freud, 1911b, p. 219) that force the newborn child to reckon with external reality. The child can urinate or defecate reflexively by himself but when it comes to being fed, he needs the provision offered

[3] In fact, Freud (1927c) included human helplessness in the face of "majestic, cruel, and inexorable" (p. 16) forces of nature among the incentives for the development of religious ideas.

by someone else (most often, his mother). He cannot satisfy his hunger by himself. The following passage by Freud (1911b) eloquently explicates this matter.

> ... the state of psychical rest was originally disturbed by the peremptory demands of internal needs. When this happened, whatever was thought of (wished for) was simply presented in a hallucinatory manner, just as it still happens today with our dream-thoughts every night. It was the only non-occurrence of the expected satisfaction, the disappointment experienced, that led to the abandonment of this attempt at satisfaction by means of hallucination. Instead of it, the psychical apparatus had to decide to form a conception of the real circumstances in the external world and to endeavour to make a real alteration in them. A new principle of mental functioning was thus introduced; what was presented in the mind was no longer what was agreeable but what was real, even if it happened to be disagreeable. This setting-up of the *reality principle* proved to be a momentous step. (p. 219, italics in the original)

This proposal of Freud was widely accepted and reiterated with changed phraseology and points of emphasis. Instead of listing these "reformulations", I will note only the important additions to Freud's notion that, sooner or later, the growing ego has to deal with the demands and restrictions of external reality and, in the process, lose its omnipotence.

Hartmann (1939) introduced the concept of "adaptation" in referring to the ego's capacity to cope appropriately and advantageously with its environment. He distinguished between "alloplastic adaptation," where the ego alters the external reality to meet its needs (e.g., via migration), and "autoplastic adaptation," where the ego modifies itself to fit in better with the environment (e.g., by learning the hitherto foreign language of one's new land). Hartmann stated that a growing child has to acquire skills for both types of adaptation.

Spitz (1953) emphasized that the infant must achieve the "reality principle" before he can perceive anything objectively. He stated that "Only when the infant becomes able to postpone the gratification of the hunger drive, communicated to him by the proprioceptor stimulus, will it become free to direct its psychic energies to its environment and to perceive the environmental world, that is, the food object" (p. 325). He went on to say that perception and thought transform the drive pressure into aim-directed activity. Aggression is then placed in the service of acquiring skills and achieving mastery, among which grasping is one of the first and locomotion the second.

Winnicott (1953) noted that with the establishment of the reality principle and thus an inner–outer distinction on the ego's part, not only a true external world is born but so is an inner reality. He went on to state that:

> … if there is a need for this double statement, there is also a need for a triple one; the third part of the life of a human being, a part that we cannot ignore, is an intermediate area of experiencing, to which inner reality and external life both contribute. It is an area which is not challenged because no claim is made on its behalf except that it shall exist as a resting place for the individual engaged in the perpetual human task of keeping inner and outer reality separate yet inter-related. (p. 90)

Winnicott emphasized "that the task of reality-acceptance is never completed, that no human being is free from the strain of relating inner and outer reality, and that relief from this strain is provided by an intermediate area of experience" (p. 96). Addressing the ontogenetic counterpart of this proposal in a later paper, Winnicott (1962) stated that "The baby can meet the reality principle here and there, now and then, but not everywhere all at once; that is, the baby retains areas of subjective objects along with other areas in which there is some relating to objectively perceived objects or 'not-me' ('non-I') objects" (p. 57).

Winnicott's notions found support in Sandler's (1960) proposal of the "safety principle." Sandler stated the process of perception transforms unorganized sensations from various sense organs into organized and structured categories. This helps distinguish situations of comfort from situations of danger. Thus, "The successful act of perception is an act of integration that is accompanied by a definite feeling of *safety*" (p. 2, italics in the original). Sandler declared that it is such "safety principle that mediates the development of the reality principle from the pleasure principle" (p. 2). In a later paper, originating from the research project known as the Hampstead Index, Sandler (1962) offered a refined view of how the ego capacities of perception and thought help in reality testing while also confirming (or refuting) the notions one holds internally.

> The ego makes use of its organized internal frames of reference to structure and control both perception and thinking, and these activities in their turn, can modify the child's internal world. In normal progressive ego-development, the child deals with contradiction and incongruity between aspects of perception and thought by restructuring his inner perceptual and conceptual models, and this restructuring facilitates adaptation. There is a fundamental tendency within the ego to resolve such contradictions, to synthesis and integration. If the outcome of this tendency to integration increases the child's ability to predict and control events more successfully, we speak of successful reality testing, and in this context we may speak of successful concept testing as well. (p. 319)

Translating such formulation into the language of object relations theory, Kernberg (1967) noted that the differentiation of self-images from object images which form part of early introjection is one of the first tasks of the growing ego. This task is accomplished

> ... in part under the influence of the development of the apparatuses of primary autonomy, which are preconditions for the operation of introjection and identification processes. Perception and memory traces, as they are stored and integrated, help to sort out the origin of stimuli and the differential characteristics of perception, and gradually differentiate self from object images. Also, the gratification of instinctual needs and their moderate frustration foster the differentiation of self images from object images, because libidinal gratification draws attention cathexes to the interaction between self and objects and fosters the differentiation in that area, and because frustration brings to awareness the painful absence of the fulfilling objects and thus contributes to differentiate self from nonself. Excessive

> gratification of instinctual needs may retard the differentiation between self and objects. From a clinical point of view, however, excessive frustration of early instinctual needs (especially oral) is probably the main cause of the lack of differentiation between self and objects, because *excessive frustration reinforces the normal disposition to regressive refusion of self and object images.* (p. 663–664, italics in the original)

Kernberg noted that excessive gratification during infancy can impair reality testing but more often it is severe frustration of early instinctual needs that leads to regressive fusion of self and object images, thus laying down the foundations of a psychotic core to the personality.[4]

Pooling together the observations cited above, it seems that renunciation of infantile acceptance and establishment of reality testing (even with the allowance for a Winnicottian "intermediate area of experience") is an important area of consensus when it comes to early childhood development.

Establishing a satisfactory bond with the mother

The unparalleled significance of a child's relationship with his or her mother was repeatedly emphasized by Freud. In an oft-quoted statement, he noted:

> ... that people who know that they are preferred or favoured by their mother give evidence in their lives of a peculiar self-reliance and an unshakeable optimism which often seems like heroic attributes and bring actual success to their possessors" (Freud, in a footnote added in 1911 to *The Interpretation of Dreams*, 1900a. p. 398)

A few years later, Freud referred to the mother as "the first love object" (1916–17, p. 329), and declared that "a child's first erotic object is the mother's breast that nourishes it" (1940a, p. 188). Without denying the significance of Freud's observations, one has to acknowledge that his

[4] For details regarding the genesis of "psychotic core," see Volkan and Akhtar (1997).

comments were made in passing. They were neither theoretically elaborated nor clinically explicated. It was left to subsequent analysts, especially Klein, Bowlby, Spitz, Winnicott, and Mahler to map out the finer details of the mother–infant relationship and its lifelong impact upon the developing mind.[5]

Klein (1935, 1940) must be credited for "replacing" Freud's largely oedipally based developmental agenda by one that focused upon the earliest mother–child unit. It is true that her "good" and "bad" mothers mostly referred to the drive-based internal representations constructed by the infant and had little to do with live, breathing, actual women. It is not true, however, that she paid no attention at all to the presence or absence of the mother or to the mother's actual behavior toward her baby. For instance, in talking about the infant's bliss in being suckled, Klein (1957) declared that this experience constitutes the basis of:

> … all later happiness and makes possible the feeling of unity with another person; such unity means being fully understood, which is essential for every happy love relation or friendship. At best, such an understanding needs no words to express it, which demonstrates its derivation from the earliest closeness with the mother in the preverbal stage. The capacity to enjoy fully the first relation to the breast forms the foundation of experiencing pleasure from various sources …. A full gratification at the breast means that the infant feels that he has received from his loved object a unique gift which he wants to keep. This is the basis of gratitude. (p. 188)

And, in elucidating the foundations of the sense of loneliness, Klein (1963) referred to the fact that:

---

[5]While the biological mother remains the focal point of these contributions and also of this text, the fact is that "maternal care" can be provided by grandmothers, adoptive mothers, foster mothers, lesbian mothers, housekeepers and nannies, and, in non-Western cultures, by sundry other female close relatives. A recent edited volume of mine, *The New Motherhoods* (Akhtar, 2016), summarizes the emergent literature in this realm.

> ... early emotional life is characterized by recurrent experiences of losing and regaining. Whenever the mother is not present, she may be felt by the infant to be lost, either because she is injured or because she has turned into a persecutor. The feeling that she is lost is equivalent to the fear of her death. Owing to introjection, the death of the external mother means the loss of the internal good object as well, and this reinforces the infant's fear of his own death. These anxieties and emotions are heightened at the stage of the depressive position, but throughout life the fear of death plays a part in loneliness. (p. 304)

Endopsychically anchored though it is, Klein's account does refer to the mother's actual presence or absence. Bowlby (1956) made the role of the actual mother even more explicit. He emphasized that while the need of the infant to attach himself to a mother figure is pre-wired for survival, it actually goes beyond physiological needs and is primarily a socially oriented drive. In his trilogy of *Attachment*, *Separation*, and *Loss*, Bowlby (1969, 1973, 1980) elaborated upon the significance of the infant's secure early attachment to the mother and the adverse consequences of the weakness or absence of such a bond. He noted that attachment is a component of a larger psychobiological system. It enhances safety through proximity, assures nourishment, and facilitates learning about the environment. A secure attachment enables growth of cognitive and social capacities. Bowlby's foundational observations were further elaborated upon and refined by the later work of Ainsworth (1967, 1989) and Beebe (1986, 2000) among others.

Spitz (1946, 1965), who had closely observed severely neglected and deprived children, traced the development of the internalized libidinal object that is fundamental to the growing child's (and later, adult's) well-being. Spitz emphasized that the emergence of the "social smiling response" around six weeks of age is the first glue that attaches the child to a loving caregiver (most often the mother). He described two other phenomena that mark a growing level of object specificity for the infant. The first of these is "separation anxiety" (around five to six months of age) which refers to the infant's panic at mother's leaving his field of vision; her visual absence is equated with her actual, total, and permanent absence and this, in turn, causes distress. The second phenomenon is "stranger anxiety" and refers to the child's distress at being handed over to (or simply, upon a close encounter with) a stranger. It is as if the child were saying, "You are not safe for me since you are not my mother." This reaction appears around eight months of age. Finally, Spitz noted the prolonged separation from mother during the first year of life has the potential to lead to "anaclitic depression" in the child. However, this is more or less preventable if the substitute caregiving figure is well-attuned and empathic to the child's needs.

The profound importance of the mother to the child's survival and functioning led Winnicott (1960a) to declare that "there is no such thing as an infant" (p. 587). Or, to put it less elusively, there is no such thing as an infant alone since a human infant exists as a member of the infant–mother dyad. Winnicott laid emphasis upon the "natural" mother and what she does "naturally." By this he meant a mother who could identify with her newborn baby via "primary maternal preoccupation (1956a)[6] and then gradually permit him to grow out of such an illusory union and become himself. Winnicott held mother's contribution to an individual's health as primary and most important.

> From my point the view, the mental health of the individual is being laid down from the very beginning by the mother who provides what I have called a facilitating environment, that is to say one in which the infant's natural growth processes and interactions with the environment can evolve according to the inherited pattern of the individual. The mother is (without knowing it) laying down the foundations of mental health of the individual. (1969, pp. 24–25)

Winnicott introduced two other important concepts in this context: (i) the "good-enough mother" (1960a) who, while not being perfect, is devoted to her child, tries to understand the child's mind, survives his assaults, almost never fails in meetings the child's ego needs though

---

[6] "Primary maternal preoccupation" refers to a maternal state that is characterized by "heightened sensitivity during, and especially towards the end of, pregnancy. It lasts for a few weeks after the birth of the child. It is not easily remembered by the mothers once they have recovered from it" (Winnicott, 1956a, p. 302).

might frustrate his id wishes,[7] and is able to leave him alone when he seems to require autonomous functioning; and, (ii) "going-on-being" (1960a) which refers to smooth unfolding of the infant's constitutionally given tendencies. It is characterized by spontaneity, authenticity, agency, and continuity. All this is made possible by the non-intrusive "holding" by the mother and by her providing the infant an "illusion" of omnipotence.

Such initial mother–child merged state was termed "symbiosis" or "symbiotic phase" by Mahler (1967). It reflected a developmental period (from about the second month to five–six months of age) in which "the infant behaves and functions as though he and his mother were an omnipotent system—a dual unity with one common boundary" (p. 78). Acknowledging that she had borrowed some of these ideas from the earlier work of Benedek (1938, 1949), Mahler emphasized that her choice of the term "symbiosis" was metaphorical and not biological. It referred to a state of psychic undifferentiation (on the infant's part) or fusion with the mother, and of lack of distinction between the inner and outer worlds. According to Mahler,

> The essential feature of symbiosis is hallucinatory or delusional, somatopsychic, omnipotent fusion with the representation of the mother and, in particular, delusion of common boundary of the two actually and physically separate individuals. (1967, p. 79)

Mahler emphasized that "mutual selection of cues" (p. 86), that indicate needs, tensions, and pleasures plays a very important role here. The infant offers many cues but the mother selectively responds to only some of them. The infant then alters his behavior accordingly. He does so in a characteristic way—"the remnant of his own innate endowment and the mother child relationship. From this circular interaction emerge patterns of behaviour that already show certain overall qualities of the child's personality" (p. 86).[8] The "circular interaction" mentioned by

---

[7] For a thorough discussion of the need–wish distinction, see Akhtar (1999b).

[8] Such rudimentary "personality" might even include a sense of gender (Greenacre, 1958). The dialectics of the baby's biological sex and messages imbued in the parental gaze plays a central role in imprinting this "core gender identity" (Stoller, 1964) on the infant.

Mahler received finer attention later by Tronick (1989, 2007), Greenspan (2007a, 2007b), A. Harrison (2012), and Harrison and Beebe (2018).

With this being said, let us take a step back and see how the various proposals outlined above fit into a larger scheme of things. To my mind, Freud's (1916–17) calling the mother the child's "first love object" (p. 329), Klein's (1935) elucidation of the formation of a "good internal object," Bowlby's (1956, 1969) emphasis upon the formative influence of "secure attachment," Spitz's (1965) "structuring" of the libidinal object, Winnicott's (1960a) "good-enough mother" permitting the "illusion of omnipotence," and Mahler's (1967) description of the infant–mother "dual unity" during the symbiotic phase—all point to one and the same thing.[9] This refers to the developmental primacy and foundational significance of the early mother–child bond. It is from this very base that the child takes his steps toward independent functioning.

Moving toward autonomy and independence

While one can certainly extract passages from Freud's and Klein's writings that apply to the child's movement from dependence to independence, this developmental step has been most explicitly addressed by Winnicott and Mahler. Winnicott (1960a) not only described such advance in detail, he also linked it with the vicissitudes of adaptation to reality and the emergence of object relations. He stated,

> One half of the theory of the parent–infant relationship concerns the infant, and is the theory of the infant's journey from absolute dependence, through relative dependence, to independence, and, in parallel, the infant's journey from the pleasure principle to the

---

However, how malleable (Money, 1955) or fixed (Kleeman, 1971) this early gender sense is, remains open to question. And, of course, an important role is played here by the later childhood influences of being given a name, parental encouragement to dress a certain way or play with certain toys, changing body physiology, subjective experience of oneself, and sociocultural expectations. With the traditional binary gender categories coming increasingly into question and with the theoretical resurgence of psychic bisexuality (for an update on this, see Gulati & Pauley, 2019), this realm of development has been thrown wide open for further research and reformulation.

[9] Erikson's (1950b) concept of "basic trust" also belongs to this realm.

> reality principle and from autoerotism to object relationships. The other half of the theory of the parent–infant relationship concerns maternal care, that is to say the qualities and changes in the mother that meet the specific and developing needs of the infant towards whom she orientates. (1960a, p. 42)

Winnicott went on to describe three stages: (i) absolute dependence (in which the infant has no control or even "knowledge" of maternal care though he is utterly reliant upon it), (ii) relative dependence (in which the infant becomes aware of the maternal care and his need for it and tries to control it), and (iii) toward independence. Describing this third step, Winnicott said,

> The infant develops means for doing without actual care. This is accomplished through the accumulation of memories of care, the projection of personal needs and the introjection of care details, with the development of confidence in the environment. Here must be added the element of intellectual understanding with its tremendous implications. (1960a, p. 46)

A few years later, Winnicott (1963b) added a nuance to the state of "absolute dependence" by saying that even there, at least conceptually, we can envision the infant to be:

> ... at one and the same time dependent and independent. It is this paradox that we need to examine. There is all that is inherited, including the maturational processes, and perhaps pathological inherited trends, and these have a reality of their own, and no one can alter these; at the same time, the maturational processes depend for their evolution on the environmental provision. (pp. 84–85)

In Winnicott's view, such environmental provision was a mandatory requirement for movement toward independence to occur. A similar perspective can be discerned in Mahler's (1967, 1972) proposal that a satisfactory "symbiotic phase" is the foundation from which the child takes his steps toward "separation–individuation." She, along with her colleagues Pine and Bergman (1975) delineated four subphases of the process ("differentiation," "practising," "rapprochement," and "on the road to object constancy") by which the infant emerges from existential symbiosis with the mother to develop his psychic separateness and individuality. The two tracks (*separation* and *individuation*) are overlapping but distinct. The former refers to the autonomy of ego function, the latter to the distinct and unique direction and texture of psychic contents.[10] The first step of the separation–individuation process is the *differentiation subphase* (from about four or five to eight or nine months), in which the child starts to learn about his psychological separateness through rudimentary explorations of the self as well as the mother's environment. Next is the *practising subphase* (from nine to 16–18 months), in which the toddler elatedly enjoys his newfound psychomotor autonomy and appears to be involved in the "conquest of the world." Then comes the *rapprochement subphase* (from about 16 to 24 months), in which the child learns that his separateness, autonomy, and motor abilities have their limits. The realities of the external world appear harsh and the child regresses in the hope of reestablishing the lost symbiotic bliss with the mother. This return, however, is ambivalent, since the drive of individuation is at work with greater force. The resulting "ambitendency" accounts for the alternating cycles of dependence and flight characteristic of a child in this phase. If overcome, the rapprochement phase is followed by a period designated *on the road to object constancy*, in which a deeper, somewhat ambivalent, but more sustained object representation is internalized, the libidinal attachment to which does not become seriously compromised by temporary frustrations. This is accompanied by a more realistic and less shifting view of the self. The attainment of "self constancy" establishes a coherent, single self-representation with minimal fluctuations under drive pressures. The attainment of "object constancy"[11] assures the mother's lasting presence in the child's mental structure.

---

[10] In the West, the two tracks are intertwined while in the East, considerable individuation is possible without comparable separation (Bonovitz, 1998).

[11] The term "object constancy" was introduced in the psychoanalytic literature by Hartmann (1952) but in current parlance, its use is mostly in the context of Mahler's separation–individuation theory.

The child who is thus capable of a wider range of affects (Blum, 2005; Tyson, 1988, 2005), optimal distance (Akhtar, 1992), independent functioning, and of relating to objects that are distinct from the self, enters the oedipal situation where the presence of the father as the "third" object acquires a profound importance. However, the role of the father is neither restricted to the oedipal phase nor reducible to the erotic realm; it is far more pervasive and complex.

Benefiting from contact with the father and the attendant triangulation

Freud had much to offer regarding the father's role in child development. Most of his observations though involved the oedipal father. In the now renowned case study of Little Hans, Freud (1909b) traced the boy's castration anxiety to his talionic dread of his father's retaliation. In *Totem and Taboo*, Freud (1912–13) speculated about the "pre-historic" origins of the father–son struggle and its impact upon the modern man's inclination toward hostile competitiveness and guilt. A few years later, he (1924d) offered a more coherent vision of the father being the object of girls' admiration and boys' hostility, as well as being the founder of the incest barrier in the family. Freud emphasized that the boy renounced his erotic longings toward the mother because of the dread of castration by the father.[12] In subsequent papers, Freud (1925j, 1930a) talked of the boy's preoedipal development including "identification of an affectionate sort with his father" (1925j, p. 251) and declared that he "can not think of any need in childhood as strong as the need for a father's protection" (1930a, p. 72).

Klein (1927) agreed with Freud's notions about the father's importance for both boys and girls. However, in later writings (Klein, 1945), she sought to modify Freud's views in subtle ways. For instance, she noted that identification with father was less conflictual for both boys and girls than identification with mother. Klein also said the following about the boy's oedipal situation: "In my experience, the Oedipus situation loses in power not only because the boy is afraid of the destruction

---

[12] Freud was unprepared to accept the suggestion by Bose (1921) that the threat of castration "owes its efficiency to its connection with the boy's wish to be a female" (p. 125).

of his genital by a revengeful father, but also because he is driven by feelings of love and guilt to preserve his father as an internal and external figure" (1945, p. 418).

With regard to the girl, too, Klein added greater texture to Freud's formulation:

> The phase in which, according to Freud, the girl is exclusively attached to her mother already includes, in my view, desires directed towards her father and covers the early stages of the inverted and positive Oedipus complex. While I therefore consider this phase as a period of fluctuation between desires directed towards mother and father in all libidinal positions, there is no doubt in my mind as to the far-reaching and lasting influence of every facet of the relation to the mother upon the relation to the father. Penis envy and the castration complex play an essential part in the girl's development. But they are very much reinforced by frustration of her positive Oedipus desires. Though the little girl at one stage assumes that her mother possesses a penis as a male attribute, this concept does not play nearly as important a part in her development as Freud suggests. (p. 418)

In contrast to the Freudian and Kleinian focus upon father's role during the Oedipus complex, Winnicott (1946) addressed his role in lending strength to the "holding" needed by the growing child. Father's limit-setting curtailed the "antisocial tendency" (Winnicott, 1956b) that, in subclinical forms, was ubiquitous in human nature. Father was the container and modulator of the child's aggression. Winnicott (1969) later refined his ideas about the father's role in child development and stated that the father is important to the child in three different ways: (i) as a separate object of early bonding, (ii) as an object that relates to the mother, and (iii) as an object that exists in the mother's mind as she is taking care of her child. In a novel twist to Klein's (1935) "part-object"–"whole object" conceptualization, Winnicott proposed that while the mother appears on the child's psychic horizon as dissociated part-objects and only later coheres into a whole object, the sequence is the opposite with the father. He appears as a fresh, whole object at first and later might be relegated to different part-object roles.

Winnicott's (1946) opening up the vista to the study of the preoedipal father was enthusiastically followed by Loewald's (1951) observation that the father acted as a protector against engulfment by the mother. Mahler (1967) emphasized that the child reacted to the father as a breath of fresh air, one who was different from mother and was more playful. Benedek (1970) addressed the ego-building role of the father and Abelin (1971) described the father's role in helping the preoedipal child separate from the mother. Such early father–son relationship also drew attention from Blos (1965, 1967, 1974, 1985), Pruett (1988), and Herzog (2001). Pruett noted that the child uses his father's body for play and testing of aggression (as against the mother's body, which is sought for nourishment and haven). Herzog coined the term "father hunger" for a growing boy's need for contact with his father in order to consolidate his own sense of masculinity; while Herzog acknowledged that such "hunger" can also exist in girls, this idea was elaborated by later analysts (see below). Blos stated that father's approval instills in the son "a modification of self-possession and self-assertion—distilled as it were, out of mutual sameness or shared maleness—which renders the wider world not only manageable and conquerable but infinitely alluring" (1985, p. 11).

The relationship between father and daughter,[13] briefly mentioned in Abelin's (1971) paper, was later elaborated upon by Tessman (1982), Bernstein (1983), Benjamin (1988), Ross (1990), Chodorow (1994), and Garfield (2004). These authors delineated the dialectics of distance and intimacy in the developmental dialogue between fathers and daughters. They noted the longing in a girl for a close and collaborative relationship that exists parallel to her oedipal desire for him.

Bernstein (1983), in a seminal contribution to the topic of female superego, described the problems faced by a growing girl—and, later, a woman—when the father is available as an object of desire and idealization but not as a model of efficacy and object for identification. In Tessman's (1982) phraseology, the girl's "erotic excitement" is validated

---

[13] While the father–son relationship has received much attention from filmmakers, there are very few movies depicting the father–daughter relationship. Four movies that come to mind are *Music Box* (1989), *My Girl* (1991), *Imaginary Crimes* (1994), and *Leave No Trace* (2018).

by such a father while her "endeavor excitement" is not. Explicating this matter further, Garfield (2004) notes that:

> The father's unique contribution here is to accept his daughter's femininity, sexuality, and her interest and competence in work. If he denigrates her endeavor excitement, and/or demands compliance as a part of her femininity, she will experience great conflict about work. If he can only value her achievements, her identity as a loving girl and woman will be comprised. (p. 41)

A girl who lacks a father supportive of both her efficacy and her erotic strivings feels hurt; the resulting anger can give rise to the defensive idealization on the one hand and helplessness and masochistic submission on the other. Benjamin (1988) has poignantly described such an impact of a missing father on female development, and Chodorow (1994) has elucidated the cultural factors operating in this realm.

Increasing cognitive sophistication

With growing age, the child acquires increasingly sophisticated cognition. The steps of such intellectual development have largely been the purview of academic psychology and the work of Piaget (1937) has reigned supreme in this realm. According to him, this cognitive development proceeds on the basis of "constructivism" or by the children's active engagement, even transformation, of their object world. As children develop knowledge, they learn patterns of activity that involve perception, sensation, emotion, and physical movement. Putting the data from these sources together, children evolve schemes and then extend those schemes to other situations. Two processes aid the advance of cognition: "assimilation" (understanding new experiences in terms of preexisting ones) and "accommodation" (changing one's perspective in light of fresh experiences).[14]

---

[14] It is hard to ignore the overlap between Piaget's (1937) concepts of "assimilation" and "accommodation" and Hartmann's (1939) views on "autoplastic" or "alloplastic" adaptations.

Piaget described four stages of cognition development: (i) *sensorimotor stage* (zero to two years of age). In this stage, self-awareness and cognizance of consequences is rudimentary. "Thinking" is mostly done via motor activity, be it is reflexive (e.g., sucking, touching, grasping), or "circular" (i.e., repetitive) with variable degrees of intentionality. Gradually, the infant begins to combine action–result schemes, and attempts to obtain desired results. Still later, if the desired result is not forthcoming, the infant attempts new ways; (ii) *preoperational stage* (two to seven years of age). This stage is characterized by consolidation of "object permanence" (knowing that the physical absence of an object does not mean its actual absence; mother's playing the "peek-a-boo" game helps in the achievement of this capacity). There are pretend play, use of simple language, and imitation of things and people even in their absence; (iii) *concrete operational stage* (seven to 11 years of age). Now logic makes its appearance. Capacity to work things out by thinking about them increases. Measuring, counting, and categorizing objects becomes possible and this, in turn, facilitates thinking about patterns in the external world, and (iv) *formal operational stage* (12 to 15 years). The child now becomes capable of forming hypotheses, testing them out, and learning from such "experiments." Trial and error become his intellectual guides, role-playing and transient identifications his teachers.

Piaget's proposals are well-accepted and continue to be the foundation of our understanding of our childhood cognitive development. Their clinical importance lies in helping us grasp that a traumatized young child is often unable to intellectually process the hurtful event. This is strikingly evident in the case of children who have lost a parent before the age of seven or eight; they cannot understand the irreversibility, nonfunctionality, and universality that characterizes death (Hoffman et al., 2010; Nagy, 1948) and continue to believe, in a part of their mind, that the dead parent is still alive. Such linkage between cognition and trauma brings up the more specifically psychoanalytic to the realm of intellectual development. The following are some prime selections from this particular aspect of psychoanalytic literature:

- *Distinction between "thing-presentation" and "word-presentation"*: The former "consists in the cathexis, if not of the direct memory images of the thing, at least of remoter memory-traces derived from these"

(Freud, 1915e, p. 201). The latter consists in the cathexis of the words representing that thing as well. The System Cs is characterized by the coexistence of thing and word presentation whereas the System Ucs is populated by thing presentations only.[15]

- *Distinction between "primary process" and "secondary process"*: Freud proposed this distinction in 1895 in his "A Project for a Scientific Psychology" (1950a) and elaborated its full details in *The Interpretation of Dreams* (1900a). The "primary process" has free-flowing psychic energy at its disposal, employs displacement and condensation, and follows the "pleasure principle"; such thinking is characteristic of dreams and wish-fulfilling fantasy life. The "secondary process" in contrast has bound energy that flows in a controlled manner, is subject to the reality principle, and accommodates the imperatives of time and logic. The functions of attention, reasoning, judgment, and thoughtful action represent the "secondary process."
- *Synthetic function of the ego*: Proposed by Hartmann (1939) this function seeks to create unity, meaning, linkage, and higher forms of abstraction. It is thus a manifestation of the "life instinct."
- *Intermediate area of experience*: This concept of Winnicott (1953) refers to a psychic terrain where reality and unreality can coexist, where playful imagination and creativity arise, where "primary" and "secondary" processes intermingle, and where paradox reigns supreme.
- *Alpha elements, beta elements, and maternal reverie as the container*: Bion (1962) proposed that there exist, in the mind, sense impressions and feeling states that represent undigested facts; these are called "beta elements." Highly vulnerable to projection, these elements are "unthinkable"; they are essentially things unto themselves. They require the reliable "container" of maternal reverie to be transformed into "alpha elements" which constitute building blocks of language and thinkable thoughts. Bion's proposal implies that while capacity for thinking is hardwired, its meaningful use is made possible only with maternal help.

---

[15] The significance of this distinction to the use of obscene words was noted long ago by Ferenczi (1911).

- *The Grid*: This refers to a complex arrangement of conceptual axes evolved, over many years, by Bion (1965, 1970) in order to organize the ways in which thinking takes place. The horizontal axis contains six named columns (definitory [sic] hypothesis, falsehood, notation, attention, research, and action) and one "open" one at its end. The vertical axis contains eight columns (beta elements, alpha elements, dream thoughts, preconception, conception, concept, scientific-deductive system, and algebraic calculus). At the risk of oversimplification, the horizontal axis can be seen as compromising elements of how to think and the vertical axis about what kind of material is being offered to be thought about. The former is the "usage axis" and the latter a "genetic axis." The "grid" is an instrument for the better understanding of steps in cognitive grasp and its interpretation.
- *O*: This is a term coined by Bion (1965, 1970) to denote the ultimate truth of the moment or for the thing-in-itself, which is immeasurable. This truth is out there, waiting to be found by a receptive mind that has emptied itself of preconception, memory, and desire. Acquired knowledge can prepare the platform from which such a leap of faith is taken, but it is leaving knowledge and experience behind that actually constitutes a step toward "O." Take, for instance, the Oedipus complex, or, for that matter, the mathematical equation $E=mc^2$; these "truths" existed long before Sophocles, Freud, and Einstein discovered them. In other words, "O" is the absolute truth and the supreme godhead of veracity. Moreover, "O" is constantly becoming; "O" of one moment may not be the "O" of the next moment. The significance of this concept for cognition resides in its implication that objective truth and even thought itself preexists the human mind; thinking is a product of the human mind, thought is not.
- *Renunciation of anthropomorphism and animistic thought*: With the exceptions of poetry, surrealistic fiction, mythology, and abstract painting, the early cognitive tendency toward anthropomorphism (i.e., interpreting nonhuman in human terms) and animism (i.e., attributing human mental qualities to animals, trees, and things of all sorts) is given up with the advancement of childhood mentation. A child can believe that when he runs, the moon, up above in the sky, runs with him; but the adult knows that this is not the case. While Freud (1911c) talked about the vicissitudes of such "primitive"

thinking in his Schreber case, it is Searles (1960) who devoted the most thorough attention to the vicissitudes of animistic thinking.

- *Concretization of thought*: This refers to a process by which abstract thinking is given up in favor of literalness and physicalistic causality. The cognitive direction shifts to loss of metaphor, decline in wit, search for external causes of one's behavior, and compromised capacity for meaningful dialogue. Arieti (1974) explored concretization in his work on schizophrenia and Grubrich-Simitis (1984) in her description of the early stages of psychoanalytic treatment of the Holocaust survivors' offspring. An aphorism that has been passed down the generations of psychoanalysts and presumably originated by Harry Stack Sullivan is: "What the infant does not have, the psychotic has lost" in the most succinct, if apocryphal, statement on "concretization of thought."
- *Mentalization*: This term appears in the work of Fonagy and Target (Fonagy, 1998, 1999; Fonagy & Target, 1997; Target & Fonagy, 1996). Also calling it the "reflective mode" of psychic functioning, these authors define "mentalization" as the capacity to reflect upon one's own thoughts and to experience mental states as representations. Mentalization evolves from the integration of the earlier mental operations called "psychic equivalence" and "pretend mode"; the former of these implies a conflation of intrapsychic and external realities and the latter a splitting-off of the two. Mentalization, in contrast, allows for linking up the internal and external realities. Its emergence and consolidation depend heavily upon the reflection of one's mental states in the context of secure play during childhood. In other words, the growing child needs the help of parents and older siblings in order to achieve the capacity for mentalization. The importance of mentalization is evident in the following ways: (i) it enables the child to see people's actions as meaningful, since they seem based upon feelings and thoughts; (ii) it creates the possibility of distinguishing between "inner and outer truth" (Target & Fonagy, 1996, p. 462). In other words, the child becomes able to conclude that simply because someone is behaving in this or that fashion does not mean that things *are* that way; (iii) it facilitates communication, since to keep others' perspective in mind improves listening, and guides responding; and, (iv) it enhances intersubjectivity and therefore deepens life experience.

- *A few other contributions*: Prominent among these are (i) Shapiro's (1979) work on psycholinguistics, (ii) Stein's (1985) ideas about the origins of the capacity for irony, (iii) Kafka's (1989) suggestion that parental tolerance of ambiguity helps the child distinguish between "contradiction" (conflicting ideas at one level of abstraction) from "paradox" (conflicting ideas at more than one level of abstraction), (iv) my own delineation of a "simplicity-contradiction-paradox" sequence (Akhtar, 1998) in the evolution of clinical material of borderline patients and its developmental prototype in maternal responses to children's thinking, and (v) Fallon and Sherkow's (2013) description of cognitive disorganization that accompanies each developmental achievement of the growing child.

  Together, the foregoing proposals demonstrate that psychoanalytic theory has not only contributed to understanding of the child's emotional growth but also enriched how his cognitive and intellectual functioning becomes nuanced and sophisticated over time.[16]

Acquiring a moral sense

The topic of human morality and its gradual accretion and refinement from childhood onwards through adolescence to adulthood is vast and has been taken up by a multitude of disciplines including general psychology, psychoanalysis, philosophy, sociology, anthropology, biogenetics, and ethology. As a result, the material offered here is far from exhaustive. In fact, it is highly selective. It only refers to the works of Piaget (1932) and Kohlberg (1981) from the perspective of general psychology and of Freud (1912–13, 1923b, 1924d, 1927c, 1930a) and Klein (1933, 1935, 1940) from the perspective of psychoanalysis; a few other contributors are mentioned, but largely in passing.

Piaget (1932) divided moral development into three stages: (i) *premoral stage*, the earliest one, which is characterized by lack of psychic intentionality and inadequate awareness of how one's actions impact others, (ii) *heteronomy stage*, which largely represents the ethics of constraints and compliance, and (iii) *autonomy stage*, which appears around

---

[16] See also Greenspan's (1980) contribution to this realm.

eight years of age and reflects the ethics of cooperation and reciprocity. Piaget correlated these stages with the increasing sophistication of a child's cognitive abilities. He postulated that as preoedipal thinking changes into operational thinking, the child becomes able to understand the concepts of equality, mutuality, the third-person perspective, and concern for others. This changes the earlier rule-bound and rigid morality into one that regards the welfare of others as a central variable.

It is along these lines, especially about morality in the interpersonal context, that Kohlberg (1981) evolved his proposals. Inspired by Piaget's work, he evolved a theory of moral development which had three levels, with each of these consisting of a two-step process: (i) *pre-conventional morality* (0–5 years of age), characterized first by obedience to external imperatives and avoidance of punishment, and then by assuring self-interest and seeking rewards;[17] (ii) *conventional morality* (5–12 years of age), characterized first by conformity to group mores and then by compliance with the rules laid down by authority figures, and (iii) *post-conventional morality* (12–19 years of age), characterized first by mutuality and reciprocity, and then by ethics that go beyond law and concern for mutual benefit. Kohlberg emphasized the role that appreciation of justice plays in the development of morality and tried to integrate advances in morality with those in the capacity for logical thought.[18] Later on, he (1984) added a fourth stage of *transcendental morality*, characterized by deeper involvement in humanity and spirituality.

Alongside these important contributions from general psychology exist the pioneering contributions of Freud (1923b, 1924d, 1927c, 1930a) and Klein (1933, 1935, 1940). Freud's view of human nature was rather dismal. He declared that "Most of our sentimentalists, friends of humanity, and protectors of animals have been derived from little sadists and animal tormentors" (1915b, p. 282), and that "Belief in goodness of

---

[17] Kohlberg's (1981) "pre-conventional morality" matches very well with Ferenczi's (1925) earlier description of "sphincter morality." Ferenczi used this term to denote a growing child's compliance with parental demands and expectations for proper control of excretory functions. Such compliance was largely in the service of gaining love and recognition from parents.

[18] Ma (2013) has recently provided a well-reasoned and finer integration of Piaget's and Kohlberg's models of moral development.

human nature is one of those evil illusions by which mankind expect their lives to be beautified and made easier" (1933a, p. 104). According to Freud, the human burden of guilt originated from the persistent unconscious impulses in the adult (passed on as a legacy of his childhood desires) to commit "the two great human crimes" (1916d, p. 333), that is, incest with the mother and parricide. The shocking phallocentrism and, frankly, a bit of idiosyncrasy, were left unquestioned by psychoanalysts for a long time after that statement was made. Think about it. In Freud's view, parricide is a great crime but what about matricide, or, for that matter, filicide or infanticide? Incest with the mother is a great crime but what about incest with the father or sibling? Perhaps the "two great human crimes" are incest and murder. But this could not be said by Freud, whose ideas about morality arose from either the "prehistoric" murder of the father of the primal horde by his sons (1912–13) or from the internalization of the paternal dictates, especially his threat of castration, in the form of the superego (1923b, 1924d). An unfortunate result of such phallocentric thinking was his declaration that the girl, not subject to the threat of castration (being already "castrated"), developed a superego that lacked "strength and independence" (1933a, p. 129) and grew up to become an adult with a "lesser sense of justice" (1925j, p. 257). Freud's views were challenged in his own lifetime by Horney (1926) and Jones (1935) and this trend gathered further momentum with the shift of psychoanalytic theory from a body-based ("instinctual") to a relationship-based ("object relations") model, the data supplied by infant and child observation, and the feminist critique of Freudian thinking. Blum (1996) has summarized the subsequent revisions of theory in the following statement:

> The female superego is now not regarded as weaker or deficient, and sex differences in structure and function are not given value judgements. Libido is not masculine, neither are passivity, narcissism, and masochism regarded as essentially feminine traits. Penis envy is no longer considered the bedrock of a woman's disappointment and necessary renunciation but has been subject to major reinterpretation. Neither masochism nor envy is confined to women nor necessarily related to the absence of a penis. (p. 5)

Instead of "castration anxiety" in women, one now speaks of "female genital anxieties" (Bernstein, 1990); these include access anxiety, diffusivity anxiety, and penetration anxiety. Instead of the girl's Oedipus complex, one now wonders about her "Persephone complex" (Kulish & Holtzman, 1998); this refers to the girl's experience of an erotic pull toward the father, and the resulting rivalry with the mother, who is also her greatest source of security. Instead of the purported weakness of the female superego, one advocates a greater relational anchor to moral judgment in women (Bernstein, 1983; Gilligan, 1982).[19]

Returning to Freud, we not only note that his views were phallocentric but were related mainly to guilt and that, too, mainly arising from oedipal conflicts of incestuous desire and hostile competitiveness. The resulting superego was harsh, even though some lip service was paid to the benevolent aspects of the superego as well (Freud, 1923b, 1924d). The command of such a superego was "Don't!" The desirable path to follow was determined by another structure, namely the "ego ideal," which was a product of the narcissistic cathexis of a future self-image (Freud, 1914c).

In contrast to such a rule-giving, strict superego derived from the oedipal phase, Klein (1933, 1935) proposed a much earlier foundation of the child's conscience. She stated that:

> The formation of the superego begins at the same time as the child makes its earliest oral introjection of its objects. Since the first imagos it thus forms are endowed with all the attributes of the intense sadism belonging to this stage of its development, and since they would once more be projected onto the objects of the outer world, the small child becomes dominated by the fear of suffering unimaginable cruel attacks, both from its real objects and from its superego. Its anxiety will serve to increase its own

[19] The girl's entry into the oedipal phase is also seen to follow a different pathway than that proposed by Freud (Parens et al., 1976). Her wish for a baby is no longer reductionistically traced to the sole determinant of her oedipal fantasies, even if these do play a role in the genesis of that desire; this wish is now seen to be more complex and multiply determined, with tributaries derived from constitutional givens, early identifications with maternal caregiving attributes, and developmentally forward longing to fill her inner space, etc.

> sadistic impulses by urging it to destroy those hostile objects so as to escape their onslaughts. The vicious circle that is thus set up, in which the child's anxiety impels it to destroy its object, results in an increase of its own anxiety, and this once again urges it on against its object, and constitutes a psychological mechanism which, in my view, is at the bottom of asocial and criminal tendencies in the individual. (1933, p. 251)

Klein suggested that the sadism of the superego is diminished as the child grows and begins to have consideration for his love objects. The ego-syntonic attacks on love objects during the "paranoid position" become ego-dystonic during the "depressive position" (Klein, 1935). A feeling of guilt (in my view, better termed as remorse) now sets in and, in turn, mobilizes reparative longings.

We can now see three major distinctions between Freud's and Klein's views of the moral functioning of the child: (i) in Freud's view moral development begins with the resolution of the Oedipus complex whereas in Klein's view it begins much earlier, (ii) in Freud's view development of castration anxiety is the source of moral restraints whereas in Klein's view concern for the love object is the source of moral restraint, and (iii) in Freud's view avoidance of "guilt" is the driving force of morality whereas in Klein's view "remorse" (though regrettably she calls it "guilt") is the motor of humility and reparative desire.[20]

Before ending this section, it must be noted that moral development of the child is also enriched by the internalization of his or her ethnic, religious, and national paradigms of "goodness," valor, and sacrifice. Through exposure to the family's cultural mores and ensuing identifications, the growing child acquires a sense of ethnicity which provides a feeling of belonging to a larger group and imparts historical continuity to the child's existence (Erikson, 1950a, 1956). A successful resolution of the Oedipus complex facilitates the child's entry into the father's universe (Chasseguet-Smirgel, 1984). The resulting idealization of the father imparts an understanding of generational differences and provides impetus for familial and communal filiation. This early ethnic sense, which

---

[20] Winnicott's (1963a) ideas about the "capacity for concern" largely follow such a Kleinian line of thinking.

may border on ethnocentricity, is diluted during adolescence, when a certain disidentification with parental mores occurs. The greater interaction with diverse social and ethnic groups during adolescence further facilitates the toning down of the childhood ethnocentrism.

Consolidating identity and capacity for romantic love

Tausk (1919) introduced the term "identity" into the psychoanalytic literature. He examined how the child discovers his self and asserted that man must, throughout life, constantly find and experience himself anew.[21] A number of Freud's ideas are also of great significance to the concept of identity as evident in some of his hypotheses regarding the ego.

> In the process of a child's development into a mature adult there is a more and more extensive integration of his personality (1921c, p. 79) … the ego is first and foremost a bodily ego (1923b, p. 26) … the character of the ego is a precipitate of abandoned object-cathexes and … it contains the history of those object choices (1923b, p. 29) … the ego ideal is … the heir of the Oedipus complex (1923b, p. 26) …. Anatomy is Destiny (1924d, p. 178) … all human individuals, as a result of their bisexual disposition and of cross-inheritance, combine in themselves both masculine and feminine characteristics. (1925j, p. 258)

To be sure, the word "identity" does not appear here, yet these brief statements do portray Freud's implicit view of the genesis and consolidation of identity. This view accommodates somatic underpinnings, psychic bisexuality, early identifications, the role of the Oedipus complex and its resolution, the ongoing synthetic function of the ego, and the moral dimension of character. What remained implicit yet palpably present in Freud's work was to be developed by Erikson (1950a, 1950b, 1956, 1958) who resurrected the term in his contributions to character

---

[21] Freud used the term "identity" in a technical sense only once (Guttman et al., 1980). This was in his address to B'nai B'rith, where he spoke of his "inner identity" (Freud, 1941e, p. 274) as a Jew.

formation. He used the term "ego identity" to denote "both a persistent sameness within oneself (selfsameness) and a persistent sharing of some kind of essential character with others" (1956, p. 102). He later dropped the "ego" prefix, in part to accommodate Hartmann's (1950) differentiation between ego and self. Erikson (1956) emphasized that identity could have many connotations and could refer at one time to "*a conscious sense of individual identity*; at another to an unconscious striving for *a continuity of personal character*; at a third, as a criterion for the silent doings of *ego synthesis*; and finally, as a maintenance of an inner *solidarity* with [the] group's ideals and identity" (p. 102, italics in the original). While he noted that identity formation is a lifelong development, with its roots going back to the earliest self-recognition, Erikson emphasized the period of adolescence in the consolidation of identity. He saw the adolescent as attempting to integrate what he knew of himself and his world into a stable continuum of past knowledge, present experiences, and future goals in order to elaborate a cohesive sense of personal feeling.

While psychological separateness had so far depended upon a secure internalization of the parent homeostatic functions (Mahler, 1967; Mahler et al., 1975; Settlage, 1994), acquisition of such separateness in adolescence requires a reverse process; this is the "second individuation process of adolescence" (Blos, 1967). Emotional disengagement from the internalized early object becomes necessary at this stage, and this, coupled with the characteristic drive upsurge of this period, results in a certain ego instability. Progressive and regressive trends alternate, at times with disturbing rapidity. Regressive trends cause clinging to earlier modes of self-expression. Progressive trends, both defensive and autonomous, herald new self-configurations. On the one hand, there is insistent disengagement from the earlier parental dictates internalized in the form of the superego. On the other, there is an equally tenacious reliance upon the values of the peer group. Trial identifications and role experimentations within the latter context, coupled with the support of a resilient family, gradually broaden ego autonomy and impart to the individual a greater sense of inner solidity.

Gender-related differences in identity development become greatly evident during adolescence (Blos, 1967; Fischer & Fischer, 1991; Money & Ehrhardt, 1972). Since adolescence fosters regression, both boys and girls retreat from oedipal conflicts and struggle with issues of control, autonomy, gender identity, and optimal distance from significant others. For the boy, the door to regressive closeness with mother is barred because it threatens his gender identity. He turns to his father and even more forcefully to his male peers for patterning his social identity. For the girl, regression to a close tie with the mother, with its attendant push–pull tensions, is more frequent. Both boys and girls alike deal with the resurgence of oedipal conflicts, but regression in object-relatedness is more frequently seen in girls.

Adolescence is also the time when sexual identity is consolidated. Renunciation of sexual aims toward primary love objects, reconciliation of active and passive sexual aims, and further synthesis of bisexual identifications facilitate this development (Blos, 1967). Blos, whose work (1967, 1984) is enormously important in shedding light on these processes, suggests that it is only during adolescence that the negative oedipal strivings are truly given up. Indeed, Blos (1984) declares that "The adult ego ideal is the heir of the negative Oedipus complex" (p. 319). However, what constitutes the negative Oedipus complex is no longer clear. In Blos' terminology, this meant a boy's love for father or the girl's love for mother. However, with the "depathologization" of homosexuality, the so-called negative Oedipus complex has come to be regarded as a "positive" phenomenon (Goldsmith, 1995).[22]

Alongside such consolidation of identity, there is an ongoing intrapsychic effort to arrive at the capacity for romantic love. Here, Freud comes to our assistance. Early on (1905d), he pointed out that the process of the choice of love object in human beings is essentially diphasic. The first move toward the object begins between the ages of two and five and is characterized by infantile sexual aims. This is brought to a halt by latency. Puberty then sets in the second, more explicitly sexual, movement toward the object. Meanwhile, the repression of the infantile sexual aims renders the earlier longings as merely an "affectionate current," thus causing a gap between it and the later-appearing "sexual current." What was implicit in this statement was developed further by Freud (1912d) when he noted "two currents whose union is necessary

[22] For a multitude of theoretical changes called for by the "depathologization" of homosexuality, see the important contribution of Roughton (2002).

to ensure a completely normal attitude in love ... These two may be distinguished as the *affectionate* and *sensual* current" (p. 180, italics in the original). The affectionate current was ontogenetically the earlier one. It arose in connection with the early bodily and psychic care provided by the primary objects, especially the mother. The second, more specifically sexual current, arrived on the scene with puberty. It had to be synthesized with the affectionate current. Romantic love could then be expressed toward non-familial objects with whom a sexual union was permissible and possible.

Two years after this contribution, Freud (1914c) addressed the topic of love from a different perspective. He now distinguished between narcissistic (arising from the ego's self-affirming needs) and anaclitic (arising from the ego's desire for the object's help-giving qualities) forms of love. In a subsequent paper, Freud (1915e) noted that a synthesis of libidinal and aggressive aims was also necessary for true, deep love. Still later, Freud (1921c) traced romantic idealization to the love object's ...

> being treated in the same way as our own ego, so that when we are in love, a considerable amount of narcissistic libido overflows onto the object ... We love it on account of the perfections which we have striven to reach for our own ego, and which we should now like to procure in this roundabout way as a means of satisfying our narcissism ... *The object has been in place of the ego ideal.* (pp. 112–113, italics in the original)

Then, in 1930, Freud again addressed the "unusual state" of being in love, stating that at the peak of such experience "... the boundary between ego and object threatens to melt away" (p. 66). While acknowledging the exaltation that accompanies love, Freud once again emphasized the potential of pain in it: "We are never so defenceless as when we love" (p. 82). He went on to note that many individuals protect themselves against the pain emanating from the loss of the love object by directing their love not to one person but to mankind in general and its cultural institutions.

In essence, Freud's view of love incorporates its origin in the earliest infant–mother experience, the necessity for the fusion of affectionate and erotic aims, the synthesis of libidinal and aggressive drives, the renunciation of oedipal strivings, and the affirmation of the ego ideal through the narcissistic strength drawn from the partner.

* * *

Having arrived at this point, let us look back and summarize what we have gathered about the psychoanalytic view of child development. It is clear that a child has to renounce omnipotence, establish a secure bond with the mother, learn from the contact with father, bear the travails of triangulation, acquire more sophisticated cognition, develop a sense of morality, consolidate identity, and deepen the capacity for love in order to achieve full psychic growth. This makes the infant into a child and a child into an adult. While all this seems to be agreed upon, our theory is not as tidy as this quick summary makes it appear.

Unresolved questions

Some areas of ambiguity and conceptual divergence owe their origin to the different vantage points (e.g., child observation, reconstructions during adult analyses) from which the developmental "data" is drawn. Other variances reflect fundamental differences in theory. Still others could be traced to variations of terminology and semantics. Regardless of their origins, these areas of uncertainty essentially subsume the following questions.

Is the concept of "primary narcissism" still valid?

The concept of "primary narcissism" was introduced by Freud in his paper, "On narcissism" (1914c). It was meant to denote an early state in which the child cathects his own self with the whole of his libido. Freud's proposal has been problematic from the time of its inception. Many reasons account for confusion. First, Freud referred to it as total cathexis of the self (ego) at one point (1914c) and as the state of life before formation of the ego (e.g., life in the womb) at another point (1916–17). Second, if the term is to designate "object-less love," then it clashes with the assertion that "primary object-love" (Balint, 1937) is present from birth onwards. Third, while prominent analytic theorists (Chasseguet-Smirgel, 1984;

Green, 1986; Grunberger, 1989; Kestenberg & Brenner, 1995) continue to use "primary narcissism" as a storehouse of libidinal energy that precludes the implosion of the self by death instinct, they are not observers of neonatal behavior which tends to suggest that object-relatedness, even if rudimentary, does exist in the earliest postnatal life. Mahler's (1967) normal "autistic phase" that preceded "symbiosis" was also a legacy of the "primary narcissism" concept but it gave way to "quasi-autistic phase" (Harley & Weil, 1979, p. xiii) and has been now relegated to heuristic obsolescence. More recent observers are divided on this issue. Novick and Novick (2002) discard "primary narcissism." Stern (1985) seems willing to accommodate that there might be less-related and more-related moments on the infant's part from birth onwards and it is the former that might represent "primary narcissism" or the psychic bedrock for "the emergence of a first adumbration of the ego" (Laplanche & Pontalis, 1973, p. 338). Parens (2016) has recently introduced the term "primary narcissistic stage" for this very purpose.[23]

Does the pleasure principle come before or after the reality principle?

This is another area of theoretical disagreement. In its "classic" version, psychoanalysis proposes that the child is governed by the "pleasure principle": interest in tension discharge, urgency, disregard of circumstances, and completely id-driven. Then various factors force the child to encounter, acknowledge, and accept reality. This leads to the emergence of a logically based, safety-respecting, capable of postponing tension discharge, ego-driven mentality called the "reality principle." These ideas were introduced and elaborated upon by Freud (1911b) and became widely accepted over time. However, a complication was added by Hartmann (1939) when he distinguished between "reality principle in a narrow sense" (akin to Freud's formulation of the concept) and "reality principle in a broad sense" (exemplifying the child's hardwired preparedness to suckle, to seek object contact, and so on). Emde's (1983) concept of the infant's "social fittedness" (p. 171) exemplifies Hartmann's

---

[23] Etezady (1995) has thoroughly discussed the developmental and metapsychological distinctions between "primary" and "secondary" narcissism.

latter point. It refers to the capacities that are present at birth and make the infant pre-adapted for participation in human interactions; these capacities include "a propensity for participating in eye-to-eye contact; a state responsivity for being activated and soothed by human holding, touching, and rocking; and a propensity for showing prolonged alert attentiveness to the stimulus features contained in the human voice and face" (p. 171).

A more dramatic break from the Freudian perspective was made by Kohut (1977) who suggested that the pleasure principle is neither primary nor ubiquitous. In his view, "pleasure principle" emerges as a degradation product when the caretaking environment fails to respect the child's age-specific reality functioning. This proposal has remote echoes of Winnicott's earlier paper on "antisocial tendency" (1956b) which declares that a child becomes greedy and outrageous not because of a regression to preexisting patterns of behavior but due to deprivation by his environment.

Is the drive theory still relevant?

The current emphasis upon object relations and intersubjectivity has resulted in sidelining the theory of instinctual drives. This, however, is not a new phenomenon. It goes back to Fairbairn's (1952) declaration that "Libido is the function of the ego. There is no death instinct; and aggression is a reaction to frustration or deprivation. Since libido is a function of the ego and aggression is a reaction to frustration or deprivation, there is no such thing as an id" (p. 224). Fairbairn was not a child analyst but his stance has seeped into contemporary developmental theory. To be sure, theoreticians such as Klein (1935, 1940), Greenacre (1953, 1960), Jacobson (1964), and Mahler (1967, 1972) include the drive perspective in their developmental formulations.[24] But, concepts like oral deprivation, anal rage, phallic assertion, castration anxiety, etc., have fallen into a considerable disuse in the current developmental

[24] For the purposes of didactic ease, I have not mentioned two important people here: Winnicott who shows much ambivalence toward the concept of instinctual drives (see Greenberg & Mitchell, 1983 for details) and Kernberg (1982) who has reformulated drives as organized affects and not inherent forces in themselves.

perspectives. On the one hand, this shift has enriched and deepened our understanding of the relational foundations of the self. On the other hand, it has deprived us of the significance of the "bodily ego" (Freud, 1923b), not only in the course of development but in clinical work with patients of all ages. Pine (1988) is a shining exception in this chorus of avant-garde theorists. He emphatically reminds us that psychoanalysis is actually comprised of "four psychologies" (those of drives, ego, object relations, and the self) and each of these adds something new to the understanding of development, mental functioning, psychopathology, analytic listening, and clinical interventions. Take a look at what Pine suggests that the drive theory offers us.

> The drive psychology alerts us always to ask (silently, in non-verbalized ways even to ourselves, but always in the background, guiding our listening): what wish is being expressed? What is the relation of the wish to consciousness? What is the fantasy, and how does it reflect a compromise between wish and defense and reality? How effective/adaptive is the defense? Can the particular anxiety be traced to this or that wish, is effectively defended against, and can the particular guilt be understood in terms of the system Cs. in relation to this or that wish? … Likewise for character: how have particular urges been transformed and meshed with defensive styles so as to contribute to characteristic and ordinarily ego-syntonic modes of function. And, related questions influence our historical-reconstructive-formulative view: what early under- or over-gratifications of particular drives (and their related wishes) have occurred, producing early fixations and tendencies to regression? Is there any evidence for genetically greater drive strength in one or another area, or for early trauma that provoked increased activity around particular drives? (pp. 578–579)

The help of such a perspective in understanding, formulating, and intervening with clinical material, regardless of whether it pertains to a child or an adult, is beyond question. Clearly, such assertion of the importance of "drive theory" goes against the *au courant* relational and intersubjective enthusiasm.

Is the core self a pristine or amalgamated structure?

Freud, who often used the terms "ego" and "self" interchangeably, famously stated that "The character of the ego is a precipitate of abandoned object cathexis ... [and] contains the history of those object choices" (1923b, p. 29). This line of thinking was hardly affected by Hartmann's (1950) insistence that we must think of "ego" and "self" as distinct, with the former standing for a specific mental agency and the latter for the whole person. Later analysts, especially Jacobson (1964) and Kernberg (1967) noted that what one was dealing with was not "self" per se but "self-representation"; one's objective characteristics did contribute but were not the sole determinant of how one psychically experienced the self. Drive activity and ego maturity also affected the self-representation. Moreover, self-representation evolved in the context of object relations and was affected by their affective coloration.[25] An important paper by Weil (1970) then underscored that the "basic core" of the individual is formed by selective maternal evocations of certain specific aspects of the child's inherent cognitive and affective propensities. The characteristics of this core persist as a fundamental layer of psyche and give texture to the later separation–individuation and oedipal developments. Lichtenstein's (1963) earlier notion of "identity theme" was along similar lines and Mahler et al.'s (1975) thorough description of the acquisition of self- and object-constancy irrefutably demonstrated that, even after self and object separation has set in, the core self continues to have qualities selectively evoked by the mother. In essence, all these theorists agree that even the most basic substrate of the self is an amalgam of the infant's hardwired potentials and the mother's epigenetic evocation of them. In the mapping out of endopsychic structures, regardless of whether they are Freudian (id, ego, superego), Kleinian (good and bad internal objects), Fairbairnian (exciting and rejecting objects, a central ego, and a split repressed ego), or Kernbergian (good and bad self- and object-representations), the self comes across as hardly monolithic and devoid of presences derived from the early interactional world.

---

[25] The same complexity applies to object representations. Elsewhere (Akhtar, 2005a) I have elucidated the forms, processes, and metabolism of internalization that turn important early figures into intrapsychic object representations.

In contrast to this stands Winnicott's view of the self. Over and over again, he portrays the child's self as pristine, something that under ideal circumstances does not need to introject or internalize anything. Any accommodation to the external world, including to his own mother, leads to the child's departure from genuine existence. Take a look at the following examples of such theorization.

> For the time being, during the birth, the infant is a reactor and the important thing is the environment; and then after birth there is a return to the state of affairs in which the important thing is the infant, whatever that means. In health, the infant is prepared before birth for some environment impingement, and has already had the experience of a natural return from a state of reactivity to not having to react, which is the only state in which the self can begin to be. (1949, p. 13)

In this passage, Winnicott locates the "self" even before birth,[26] hence free from environmental input. A few years later, Winnicott (1952) wrote the following: "By good enough child care, technique, holding, and general management, the shell becomes gradually taken over and the kernel (which has looked all the time like a baby to us) can begin to be an individual" (p. 99).

Winnicott's self is like a seed of a rose which would bloom into a full-fledged flower if properly cared for by a devoted gardener. However, the color of the flower and the number of its petals is not decided by that gardener. In Winnicott's (1963a) words "The environment does not make the child … [It] enables the child to realize potential" (p. 85). Such a self is a far cry from the self that is a precipitate of abandoned object cathexis. To be sure, Winnicott does allow for a state of "primary unintegration" (1945) but the three processes he describes (integration, personalization, and idealization) for that state to lead to a coherent self

---

[26] Psychic life during the intrauterine period was regarded by Freud (1918b) to be a product of "retrospective fantasizing" (p. 102). However, Balint (1968), in his revised view of the toddler's "philobatism" invoked intrauterine pleasure as this attitude's original prototype. Grunberger (1989) traced the narcissist's search for omnipotence to the dimly remembered intrauterine bliss. Such notions lend some credence to Winnicott's theorizing. More recently, Piontelli's (1987, 1992) investigations of the fetus's responses to external stimuli give additional support to this line of thinking.

are largely internal; the mother only needs to provide "holding" and preclude "impingements" for these internal processes to unfold. Such emphasis upon the solipsistic nature of the self is nowhere more clear than in Winnicott's (1960b) view of the "True Self" which has a "secret life" (p. 143). At the same time, "Only the True Self can be creative and only the True Self can feel real. Whereas a True Self feels real, the existence of a False Self [which evolves in response to the environmental demands] results in feeling unreal or a sense of futility" (p. 148).

Winnicott asserts that the True Self represents psychosomatic unity, a smooth "going-on-being" (1960a), and has its essence in living. It cannot be described. In fact, it exists incognito. Moreover, True Self is consolidated by mother's empathic decoding of the child's gesture, not by her input. The latter leads the child to become reactive and develop a False Self. And, however "adaptive" this False Self might become, its main purpose is to "search for conditions which will make it possible for the True Self to come into its own" (1960b, p. 143). Remote echoes of Winnicott's pristine, private, and primary nature of the self can be discerned in Kohut's (1977) self psychology. Together, these two perspectives stand in sharp contrast to the customary notion of the self (even at its core) being an amalgam of inherited potentials and their selective evocations by the environment.

Does development proceed according to "stages" and "phases" or get preserved as "positions"?

Freud's descriptions of oral eroticism (1905d) and anal eroticism (1908b) were initially just that: elucidations of the sensual pleasures derived from acts of sucking and defecating (as well as retaining fecal matter). The focus was upon the erotogenic zones and their aims; the object of these aims received less attention. Gradually, however, the notion of a "pregenital" organization of libido and its objects came about (Freud, 1912–13). In later revisions of *Three Essays on the Theory of Sexuality* (Freud, 1915e, 1924d), the anal stage appeared as one of the three pregenital organizations: oral, anal, and phallic. It was, however, Abraham (1924a, 1924b) who categorized these observations into a detailed scheme of oral erotic and oral sadistic stages that preceded the anal erotic and anal sadistic stages. The classification was based upon the attitude toward the object. The oral erotic stage reflected a loving and pleasurable infant–mother tie, whereas the oral sadistic stage included aggression toward the breast/mother. Similarly, the anal erotic stage focused upon the pleasure of defecating and giving the fecal "gift" to the mother whereas the anal-sadistic stage involved fecal withholding and teasing intent toward the mother. Such sequentially progressive unfolding of psychosexual development became accepted as the heuristic norm in early psychoanalysis. The oral and anal phases were seen as the precursors of the phallic-oedipal stage; the phallic subphase being about penile and clitoral masturbation, assertiveness, and exhibitionism, and the oedipal period being about insertive (active and/or passive) aims involving the parental genitalia.[27]

This line of thinking found a non-sexual counterpart in Anna Freud's (1981) delineation of the step-by-step evolution of ego functions from their infantile origins through their immature forms to their mature adult versions. She proposed that such progression depends upon the proper integration of drives, superego attributes, and environmental influences. Anna Freud elucidated such "developmental lines" for ownership of one's body, love and sex, ability to work, and capacity to establish peer relationships. Later, the realms of language acquisition (Edgecumbe, 1981), negation (Litowitz, 1998), mutuality (Bergman & Fahey, 1999), relationship with the inanimate surround (Akhtar, 2003b), and privacy (Novick & Novick, 2019) were also described along their own "developmental lines." Even Kohut's (1971) "pre-self psychology" schematics of the narcissistic sector of personality growth was based upon this Anna Freudian legacy.

A corollary of viewing development through the lens of linear progression is the conceptual duo of "fixation" and "regression." The former concept was originated by Freud (1905d) to denote a persistent attachment to pregenital aims that leads to sexual perversions. Gradually, however, the "fixation" acquired a broader connotation and came to include not only an erotogenic zone and a pregenital aim but also the entire complex of self and object relations (and their attendant affects and fantasies) from an early developmental period. The latter concept, that of "regression" (Freud, 1912–13) referred to the resurgence of earlier, primitive, and unconscious modes of relating and functioning.

---

[27] For encyclopedic coverage of the early literature on such matters, see Fenichel (1945).

All such "stage," "phase," "developmental line," "fixation," and "regression" type of notions have been put into question by Klein's (1935, 1937, 1940), Winnicott's (1960a), and latter day Kohut's (1977) developmental proposals. To be sure, Klein (1937) seems to propose a sequential progression of the capacity for peer relationships and friendships and does speak of a genital "phase" (1945) but her central organizing structures, namely "paranoid" and "depressive" "positions," are not referred to as "phases." True, that "paranoid position" develops before the "depressive position" but it does not replace the latter. In fact, the two "mentalities" (with their concomitant fantasies, affects, and cognitive postures) exist side by side throughout life. During adulthood, just as during childhood, one can respond to a given external or internal stimulus from a "paranoid" or a "depressive" position, that is, from haughty entitlement, confidence, envy and greed, or from humility, gratitude, and reparative inclination. And, to be quite clear about it, "paranoid position" is not always pathological and "depressive position" is not always healthy. A proofreader, a tax auditor, and a prosecuting attorney benefit from the deployment of the "paranoid position." A melancholic lands in difficulty from excessive reliance upon a "depressive position." The main point is that these positions exist in a parallel and not sequential manner in the mind.

Winnicott's (1956b) and Kohut's (1977) perspectives on delinquency, outrageousness, and sexually perverse activities have put the concept of "fixation" and "regression" into doubt as well. They view the emergence of the so-called "primitive" phenomena not as a return to developmental steps taken earlier (i.e., from A-B-C-D to D-C-B-A), but as an entirely new occurrence with no prior prototypes (i.e., from A-B-C-D to M-N-O-P). Together, the Kleinian proposal of mental "positions" and Winnicottian and Kohutian view that the pleasure principle is not primary but a degradation product create doubt about the veracity of a "phase"- or "stage"-based perspective on child development.

How is early childhood development affected by culture?

Almost all psychoanalytic observations regarding child development have been made in the Western context. All great child analysts have been white and so have the children they observed, treated, and wrote about. When cultural differences did exist between them and their subjects, they were overlooked in favor of the similarity of skin color and common European heritage.[28] The results of such "lily-white psychoanalysis" were generalized and upheld as norms. In talking of Eastern patterns of child-rearing, it was common to use phrases such as "too much skin-to-skin contact between mother and baby," "prolonged oral phase," "enmeshed identity," "undue reverence towards authority," and so on. African Americans were totally ignored. Worse, little awareness existed about such attitudes being naïve, condescending, and theoretically imperialistic.

Erikson (1950a, 1950b, 1959) was the sole exception to this tendency. He accorded great importance to the sociocultural influence upon the unfolding of the child's growth. He emphasized that the challenges faced and the rewards reaped by the ego, at each step of its maturation, emanated not only from within the individual but from the micro (family) and macro (school, workplace) communal realms. He set a trend and gradually more attention began to be paid to "cultural" variables in child development. This was also forced by the changing framework of the American family and American society at large. Note the following passages by Kramer (1998).

> Over the last 45 years of practicing adult and child psychoanalysis, I have noted many significant changes in the structure of the American family as well as in its child-rearing methods. When I began my practice, few mothers worked. There were also relatively few single-parent families, especially among the white population. This is no longer true, and we are seeing increasing, even alarming, numbers of single-parent families in the lower-class and lower middle-class white population. We are also seeing a rapidly diminishing number of mothers who are able to (or who choose to) stay home throughout the early formative years of their children's lives. The rise of the working mother has necessitated day-care and pre-school programs and, in more affluent circumstances, the use of nannies. All these practices have a considerable influence on childhood development. (p. 4)

[28] Many, if not most, émigré child analysts worked with children of different cultures but ignored this dimension of their work. Spitz and Mahler, Viennese and Hungarian respectively, worked with American children. Anna Freud, who was born and raised in Vienna, did most of her work in England.

Kramer went on to say that:

> Recently, a new phenomenon has also come to light. Working mothers tend to defer pregnancy until their careers are well established. Consequently, they do not become pregnant until they are into their late thirties or even forties. Often there is difficulty in conceiving, and the couple seeks to adopt a child. In either case, many newborns end up having older mothers and older fathers. The influence of this upon the growing child's ego needs further investigation. In my own child analytic experience, the situation tends to cause frequent problems. This is especially so since our culture is given to rapid changes, and the ego skills of older parents are much further removed from what a growing child needs to acquire to encounter his world in an efficacious way. (p. 4)

Two other variables led to a "cultural rejuvenation of psychoanalysis," hence that of psychoanalytically informed child developmental studies. One has to do with the demographic shifts occurring with great rapidity all over the Western world, especially the United States. It is commonplace now for American child analysts to see children of diverse races, nationalities, religions, and cultural backgrounds. This necessitated the consideration that "normal" development can have many forms that do not fit with the handed-down Eurocentric paradigms. The second source of expansion and enrichment of developmental theory arose from the arrival of psychoanalysis in the Eastern hemisphere. Clinicians and theoreticians from those regions of the world did not accept the Western developmental models *in toto* and added their own "native" observations. The following are examples from three such countries.

- *From Japan*: Takeo Doi (1962, 1989) introduced the term "amae" in the psychoanalytic literature. It denotes an intermittent, recurring, culturally patterned interaction in which the ordinary rules of propriety and formality are suspended, allowing people to receive and give affectionate ego support to each other (Doi, 1962, 1989; Taketomo, 1999). Daniel Freeman (1998), a North American psychoanalyst with extensive knowledge and experience of Japanese culture, regards "amae" to be an "interactive mutual regression in the service of ego, which gratifies and serves the progressive intrapsychic growth and development of both the participants" (p. 47). While echoes of early maternal refueling of a growing child's ego can be discerned in it, the interaction typical of amae extends beyond childhood to spread over the entire life span of the individual. In a more recent paper, Freeman (2009) has elucidated the nuances of amae in Western societies.

- *From India*: Sudhir Kakar (1989) proposed the concept of "maternal enthrallment," which refers to a complex unconscious attitude that underlies the overt idealization of the Hindu mother by her son. Kakar stated that disengagement from the overwhelming mother, and not the customary Oedipus complex, is the hegemonic narrative of the Hindu male development. On the one hand, the mother is exalted and the son is willing to follow all her commands. On the other hand, he, mostly unconsciously, wishes to break the chains, briefly, and destroy the mother. Such hostility is not only a reaction to the mother's engulfing posture (and the son's own desire for merger) but also a defense against incestuous longings that are intensified due to the great tenderness existing between them and due to the father's relatively weak role in the family.
- *From China*: Ming Dong Gu (2006) proposed that oedipal themes in China are configured by Confucian morality and take the disguised form of parental demands for filial piety and children's commitment to the resulting duties. The manifestations of such "filial piety complex" include (i) the mother's possessiveness toward her son coupled with a strong antipathy toward his wife, (ii) the son's profound longing for a woman who is a surrogate mother or an aunt with complete obliteration of the parricidal dimension of the usual Oedipus complex, (iii) the daughter's fears and blind loyalty to her father, often accompanied by an "incomprehensible inhibition against love and marriage" (p. 189). In essence, the Chinese Oedipus complex is muted, fragmented, and couched in terms of family roles and moral duties. The libidinal dimension is accentuated and aggression minimized, though it certainly lurks under the surface.

What these observations teach is this: psychoanalytic developmental theory is highly culture-dependent. Instead of imposing its Eurocentric and phallocentric norms, it needs to accommodate fresh observations without reflexively declaring them pathological. And, the mourning of a monolithic developmental scheme should be accompanied by enhancement of our own perspectives. Questions should be raised and answers should be sought. Should a baby sleep with the parents for a few months after birth or even the entire first year of life? Is a "transitional object" (Winnicott, 1953) an artefact of Western child-rearing which enforces a rapid separation between baby and mother? While "triangulation" might be inevitable and even salutary, are child, mother, and father the only dramatic personae involved in this drama or can an uncle or grandfather play the "third" role? How much regression is "permissible" once a developmental stage seems to have been mastered? And so on. Clearly, much further work is needed in this realm but this need can only be addressed if the provincialism of our developmental models is recognized first.[29]

Coda

The journey from a psychically inchoate infancy to coherent adulthood, with its sense of identity and agency, involves many steps, challenges, twists and turns, and psychosocial tasks. While areas of disagreement and uncertainty exist, there is a reasonable amount of consensus on the major nodal points of child development. It is agreed upon that the mind has to evolve distinction between self and its objects, renounce omnipotence and magical thinking, learn to bear ambivalence, acquire self- and object-constancy, negotiate travails of the oedipal situation, enter the temporal order of life, master task orientation, learn to play, reconfigure primary internal objects and one's relationship with them, merge affection and sex together, and develop capacities for intimacy, industry, and generativity. This task-filled journey to assuming adulthood takes more than two decades and demands patience from both the traveler and his or her tour guides. Neither growing-up nor child-rearing can be rushed. These processes depend upon preprogrammed epigenetic sequences

[29] In order to dispel such provincialism, I have edited psychoanalytic books on the cultures of India (Akhtar, 2005b), Australia and New Zealand (Hooke & Akhtar, 2007), the Islamic world (Akhtar, 2008), China, Japan, and Korea (Akhtar, 2009c), African Americans (Akhtar, 2012), and Hispanic Americans (Akhtar & Margery Bertoglia, 2015).

that unfold from within and facilitating psychosocial inputs that come from the outer world. And, all this takes place at its own merry pace with both progressive and regressive trends competing to take control of the developing ego.

While generally satisfied with this wide-ranging discourse on child development and its foregoing summation, I remain aware of having omitted two important realms, namely, the latency phase and the importance of sibling relationships. Allow me, therefore, to make some brief comments on them.

Latency phase

This refers to the period of childhood from six to twelve years that follows the oedipal phase and extends until the onset of puberty. It is characterized by diminution in drive energy, increasing relationships with peers, growth in ego functions, especially skills and sublimations, and by conformity to the rules of the family and community. The intense attachment to the parents is resolved and repressed. Adults outside the family (e.g., school teachers) and other children, especially those of the same sex, assume a greater role in the child's life. There is also a sublimation of sexual curiosity into intellectual curiosity, leading the child to become "calm, pliable, and educable" (Sarnoff, 1976, p. 43). Formal as well as improvised games preoccupy the child. Though largely in the service of ego mastery, the insistence on rules and fairness in such games betrays their elaborate defensive nature (Smolen, 2006). Struggle against masturbation also plays an important role in latency. Bornstein (1951) divided latency into early (from 6–8 years) and late (from 8–12 years). Williams (1972) divided "latency phase" into early latency, latency proper, and late latency subphases. However, neither of these schemes implies a strict categorization, though they do imply differences in the structural consolidation of the personality.

Sibling relationships

Freud (1900a) noted that "The older child ill-treats the younger, maligns him and robs him of his toys; while the younger is consumed with impotent rage against the elder, envies him and fears him, or meets his oppressor with the first stirrings of a love of liberty and the sense of justice" (p. 202). Despite Freud's eloquence, "sibling relationship" did not receive much attention from subsequent analysts. Feelings and fantasies involving siblings were regarded by them as mere displacements from the relationship with parents. Gradually, however, analysts began to realize that the sibling relationship can have meanings and effects of its own (Ainslie, 1997; Balsam, 1988, 1989; Colonna & Newman, 1983; Kernberg & Richards, 1988; Neubauer, 1983; Parens, 1988; Provence & Solnit, 1983; Shapiro, 1999; Solnit, 1983; Volkan & Ast, 1997). While a panoply of emotional configurations, including "twinning reactions," "womb fantasies," and "oedipal sibling triangles" were described, the one that has received the most attention is "sibling rivalry." This consists of aggressive competition between siblings for the love of their parents. The extent of sibling rivalry and, indeed, the overall flavor of the relationship between siblings depends upon the following factors: (i) parental availability, (ii) relationship between parents, (iii) parental behavior toward their children, (iv) twinship, (v) sex of the siblings, (vi) age difference between siblings, (vii) their birth order, and (viii) the existence of something "special" (e.g., extraordinary talent or, conversely, an illness) in a sibling (Akhtar & Kramer, 1999).

With these passages filling the two gaps that I found in my discourse, I wish now to conclude by bringing up a few questions that are frequently asked by our patients, their families, colleagues in non–mental health related fields, our friends and neighbors, and the public at large. These questions include the following:

- How long should one wait after giving birth to have another child?
- How long should a mother stay home after having a child before returning to her full-time employment?
- For how many days can one safely leave a one-year old child with other caregivers and take a brief holiday from parenting?
- An immigrant colleague is starting her residency in internal medicine and is considering sending her eighteen-month-old child to her parents "back home" in India for the next two years. Would this traumatize her child?
- What should a parent tell his or her five-year-old who is openly masturbating?

- What is a good answer to give to a child who asks "How did the baby get inside mommy's tummy?"
- Why can't fathers be totally responsible for the care of their babies?
- Can gay and lesbian couples be good parents to children of either sex?
- Is an adolescent who never disagrees with his or her parents normal?

Putting the protective cover of theoretical subtlety and feigned humility aside, if today's psychoanalysts can give satisfactory and confident answers to such questions, I would think that the psychoanalytic study of child development has truly come of age and yielded good results, even for those clinicians who, in the words of Helen Meyers, have merely been "hanging out with child analysts"!

CHAPTER THREE

From young adulthood through midlife to old age and death

Freud's speculations about personality development were given further substance, depth, and nuance by the subsequent works of Klein, Bowlby, Winnicott, Mahler, and their exponents (see the preceding chapter). While immensely rich, this body of literature was restricted to the unfolding of infantile and childhood psychic growth. It was left to Erikson (1950b, 1959, 1982) to push the developmental schedule farther into the human life span and to demonstrate that personality keeps evolving, changing, and growing, not only through adolescence but throughout the subsequent adulthood and even during old age. A number of investigators, especially Cath (1965, 1997), Lidz (1968), Ross (1975, 1994), Vaillant (1977), Levinson et al. (1978), Colarusso & Nemiroff (1979, 1981), Colarusso (1981, 1990, 1997), and Quinodoz (2010) then furthered the study of what came to be called "adult development." Operating in unison with Erikson's proposals, the work of these psychoanalysts set the groundwork for recognizing and accepting that (i) psychic growth is a lifelong process, (ii) the post-adolescent period can be divided into three phases, namely, young adulthood, midlife, and old age, and (iii) each of these phases presents its own challenges and demands an admixture of "autoplastic" and "alloplastic" adaptations to them. How well or how poorly an individual will tackle the multitude of such challenges depends upon the four variables identified by Clausen (1972), a Berkeley sociologist at the Institute of Human Development. These include:

> (1) The opportunities available to him or the obstacles he encounters as these are influenced by his social class, ethnic membership, age, sex, as well as the effects of war, [economic] depression, and major social changes; (2) investments of effort that the individual makes on his behalf; (3) the sources of support and guidance that help to orient him to his world and to assist him to cope with it, and (4) the personal resources the individual can command. (p. 461)

The interplay of such variables with the epigenetically unfolding sequence of adult life epochs constitutes the focus of this chapter. It aims to cover the large terrain of adult development, the literature on which is scattered and not synthesized into a composite whole. The chapter will be divided into three major sections, each representing a different area of adult life and each consisting of subsets of psychosocial tasks. Before beginning such discourse, however, it is important to note a few reservations about the undertaking.

Some caveats

First and foremost, it must be acknowledged that this essay is somewhat culturally biased. The chronological periods, psychosocial tasks, and modal portraits of young, middle, and late adulthood described in it reflect a white North American-centric bias. This limitation is in part due to my clinical experience but mostly owing to the fact that almost all literature in this realm is derived from clinical or anthropological observations involving white North American samples. Such bias restricts universal applicability of the ideas presented in this chapter and needs to be rectified by later, more culturally inclusive works. This narrative might also be heteronormative and cisgender inclined. While I have attempted, from time to time in this discourse, to insert comments and footnotes to compensate for these shortcomings, their coverage might still be suboptimal. Further contributions to rectify this deficit might be warranted.

Second, the age groups assigned to young adulthood (twenty-five to forty-five years), midlife (forty-five to sixty-five years), and old age (sixty-five till death) are not watertight compartments. These chronological boundaries are derived from the works of the authors mentioned above. While generally valid, such time frames might vary depending upon geocultural conditions, especially the average life expectancy in a given region and era.

Third, since psychoanalytic literature on "adult development" is meager (as compared to that on child development), I have had to fill in many conceptual blanks myself. That such freedom encourages both creativity as well as some intrusion of personal predilections goes without saying.

Finally, it must be emphasized that adult development does not begin *de novo*. It builds upon the foundations laid down by hereditary predispositions, childhood identifications, and adolescent transformations. Each step of adult development builds upon the preceding one, with the individual constantly evolving and changing in the process. To put it in stark and plebeian terms, becoming the parent of a first child is not the same as becoming the parent of a second or third, starting the first job differs from starting a subsequent job, and there are major differences in getting married for the first time and getting married a second time. The point is that the love–hate economy in the inner world, the ego resilience, the adaptive skills, and the social network available to the individual keep changing with time and alter his or her handling of the psychosocial challenges posed by unfolding life events. While it is true that the more loving and secure the childhood one has had, the better will be the coping strategies and outcome with advancing age (Vaillant, 1977; Levinson et al., 1978), at the same time, one cannot overlook that life is full of surprises. New people who are helpful arrive at one's threshold. Serendipitous opportunities arise. And, unexpected twists and turns await one at each step of psychic growth and maturation. That being said, we may now direct our attention to the three phases of adult and the specific joys and tensions associated with them.

Young adulthood

The phase of young adulthood begins as the "second individuation process of adolescence" (Blos, 1967) comes to its closure. Though no hard and fast rules can be laid down, generally speaking the time period between twenty-five and forty (or even forty-five) is subsumed under the rubric of "young adulthood." Like the latency-age child who has mastered separation–individuation and the Oedipus complex becomes free to explore the world of tangible and actual objects, the young adult is freed of angst-filled trial identifications of adolescence and is ready to engage with the intricacies of mature love and enter the societal workforce. He must now shift the center of gravity of his life from being a child in his family of origin to the position of a responsible individual with a new home base (psychic and actual) that is more or less his own. Four major tasks face him: (i) consolidating a life dream, finding a mentor, and establishing a work identity; (ii) assuming the role of a wage-earner and "householder", (iii) enjoying sex, love, and marriage, and (iv) becoming a parent and partaking of its attendant pleasures and responsibilities. Comments on each of these matters now follow.

Consolidating a life dream, finding a mentor, and establishing a solid identity

With the onset of young adulthood, the vacillating and often contradictory fantasies regarding one's future place in society are gradually renounced. Three important tasks now arise: (i) consolidating a life dream and giving it an actual shape in one's lived experience, (ii) finding a mentor, and (iii) making a decisive vocational choice. The so-called "life dream" (Levinson et al., 1978) refers to an imaginary scenario for one's future existence that is "more formed than a pure fantasy, yet less articulated than a fully thought-out plan" (p. 91). Levinson and colleagues state that the "life dream" has

> … the quality of a vision, an imagined possibility that generates excitement and vitality. At the start it is poorly articulated and only tenuously connected to reality, although it may contain concrete images such as winning the Nobel Prize or making the All-Star team. It may take a dramatic form as in the myth of the hero: the great artist, business tycoon, athletic or intellectual superstar performing magnificent feats and receiving special honors. It may take mundane forms that are yet inspiring and sustaining: the excellent craftsman, the husband-father in a certain kind of

> family, the highly respected member of one's community. Whatever the nature of his Dream, a young man has the developmental task of giving it greater definition and finding ways to live it out. (p. 91)

Such a dream might be passionately pursued in its literalness, modified to fit one's realities, or totally dropped and replaced by another more plausible and sustained pathway for oneself. Its evolution and working-through are, however, essential steps in the firming-up of a sense of adulthood. The sense of mastery and agency is strengthened further by breaking the dream down into its step-by-step components and, over time, translating them into real action.

This brings up the profound importance for the young adult to find a mentor. This is an older and more experienced person who is adept at dealing with the external reality. He or she becomes a development-facilitating object that helps consolidate the cognitive and social facets of the young one's work-related identity. The relationship between a mentor and her or her protégé is a special one and suffused with excitement, mutual admiration, and the healthy narcissism of a dyad. There is a shared sense of purpose between them, with the mentor facilitating the protégé's work, achievement, and success in a largely non-exploitative manner. In the book, *The Seasons of a Man's Life,*[30] Levinson et al. (1978) state:

> Mentors are essential others who strengthen the resolve to work at difficult tasks … In a "good enough" mentoring relationship, the young man feels admiration, respect, appreciation, gratitude, and love for the mentor … The elder has the qualities of character, expertise, and understanding that the younger admires and wants to make part of himself. The young man is excited and spurred on by the shared sense of his promise. (p. 100)

Elsewhere (Akhtar, 2003a), I have elaborated further on this and carved out similarities and differences between a mentor on the one hand,

---

[30] *The New York Times* bestseller, *Passages* (Sheehy, 1974), though published before Levinson et al.'s (1978) book, was actually based upon the latter's studies that had appeared in their preliminary forms as papers and research reports.

and a teacher, a parent, a lover, or a psychotherapist on the other hand. Like a teacher, the mentor imparts knowledge, clarifies underlying principles, and enhances the protégé's skills. However, a mentor is more than a teacher. He or she undertakes a task larger than transfer of knowledge: exciting the student, recognizing unevoked potentials, nurturing talent, and sponsoring the student toward the outer organizational limits of the latter's vision. Like a parent, the mentor is supportive, available for help in urgent situations, and peacefully accepting of the "forward projection of [the protégé's] narcissism" (Chasseguet-Smirgel, 1984, p. 21). And, like a parent, a mentor lets his youthful "offspring" surpass him without hurt or retribution. At the same time, a mentor is not a parent. He takes far less responsibility for extra-vocational variables of money, place of residence, and family conflicts. Talking of the last-mentioned, a mentor often creates a modicum of healthy separation from the primary objects of internal entanglement. The mentor also shows similarities with a lover and a therapist. Like a lover, he offers an exciting bond and creates a mutual product (e.g., a scientific project, a co-authored paper) that stands for a baby. However, romance and sexuality, the cornerstones of relationship between lovers, exist between the mentor and protégé only on an aim-inhibited and sublimated basis; these are not acted upon. Finally, like a therapist, the mentor listens, accepts, and transforms, but unlike a therapist, the mentor does not "interpret" or reconstruct the childhood origins of his student's fears and aspirations.

With the combination of such auxiliary ego support (by an older person) and the reformulation of the life dream (into a realistically operational plan), the young adult is prepared to make a definitive vocational choice. Now, we know that "occupation and personality traits are intimately related" (Lidz, 1968, p. 392) and those who choose professions that best synthesize their inherent temperament, accrued ego attributes, and development-based healthy identifications are indeed fortunate. A solid "work identity" (Levine, 1997) becomes both an expression of and a vehicle for a consolidation of one's overall self.

> Work furnishes the individual with an important proving ground for self-cohesion, self-definition, and adaptive competency. It is a rich and vital meeting place for the intersection and creative

> integration of inner and outer reality. How one works reflects and contributes to the fundamental ego activities of adaptation and synthesis. Work is a mainstay and measure of self-esteem and an integral component of the processes that influence the definition and creation of the self. (p. 147)

Once settled in the workplace, the young adult must form productive bonds with coworkers and "bosses." The ecosystem of the workplace becomes an extended social network. Just as trust permeates a network that brings people together, it must also be found in the workplace among coworkers. A young adult can build a reputation for being "trustworthy" when he (or she) follows through on tasks. As the career progresses, reliance upon seniors diminishes and the need to outsource tasks to others arises; this requires an ability to trust that one's subordinates will indeed finish the tasks assigned to them. Interestingly, a degree of trust must often be present in society at large to enable proper engagement with a career. Unstable political societies often breed distrust and lack of motivation. If people cannot trust that their work will have expected and good consequences, they often disengage and become indifferent. Indeed, no young adult builds an exciting career without knowing that success is an achievable and worthy goal. Such "confident expectation" (Benedek, 1938) is drawn from gratifying childhood experiences and is nurtured by the reassuring political and economic realities of the organization one works for (Sievers, 2003). Not surprisingly, then, those belonging to ethno-racial minorities and LGBT groups face greater hardship at the workplace. Besides facing frequent discrimination and "micro-aggressions" (Pierce, 1970), they also have to force their way against the "glass ceiling" imposed on their success by the majority and often, tragically, internalized by themselves (Holmes, 2006a, 2006b).

Assuming the role of a wage-earner and "householder"

As the period of formal education or apprenticeship ends and vocational choice becomes clear, the young adult enters the life phase characterized by earning money, acquiring material possessions, setting up a place of residence, and devoting himself to the pleasures and preoccupations of domestic life. In Hindu ethics, this period is one of the four phases of life[31] and is called *Grahastha*, an expression derived from combining two Sanskrit words: *grah* (home, or family residence) and *astha* (devoted to, or occupied with). Generally speaking, this is the time of getting married, starting a family, and enjoying worldly pleasures. Making money therefore becomes necessary and adds the role of a wage-earner to one's self-representation.

Such transformation unleashes many emotional challenges. On the positive side, it enhances the scope of "efficacy experiences" (Wolf, 1994) which, in turn, strengthen the ego and provide a sense of vitality to the self. The conventional acquisitions of young adults (e.g., a new car, music system, flat-screen television, home furnishings) now populate the psyche and help gratify competitive and exhibitionistic impulses while also buttressing identifications (and, dis-identifications) with parental esthetics and economic status. An opportunity for further individuation is thus created. Having one's own residence, one's own "things," and one's own money diminishes dependence upon parents, which helps solidify ego identity further and increases freedom from the internalized superego dictates. Creating one's own home and family also puts the young adult (and the couple) in assertive contrast and distinction from the surrounding group of family members and community at large. The sense of "we-ness" (Bergman, 1980) offered by the couple's smooth functioning enhances the young adult's narcissism. Advancement at the workplace and increase in income also bolster self-esteem. However, as the popular saying declares: "There is no such thing as a free lunch"; this upward climb has its own price.

> The experience of advancement and success is always based to some degree on illusion. Even when a man is doing well in an external sense, he may be gaining rewards that will turn out to

[31] These four phases are: (i) *Brahmacharya* (childhood, adolescence, and young adulthood where acquiring knowledge and staying celibate are required), (ii) *Grahastha* (the period of sexuality, material acquisition, and parenthood), (iii) *Vanprastha* (leaving home altogether and leading a hermit-like life of contemplation), and (iv) *Sanyasa* (the phase of giving up all attachment and relegating responsibilities to the younger generation).

> have little meaning or value for him. His life may provide genuine satisfactions but at great inner costs. In order to devote himself to certain goals, he may have to neglect or repress important parts of the self. Finally, a man's strivings for advancement are often stimulated by a fantasy that has the magical qualities of a fairy-tale: "If I get to the top of my ladder, I will have everything I really wanted and will live happily ever after." This omnipotent fantasy is rarely conscious during the Becoming One's Own Man phase, though it is evident to others. The man himself may become aware of it during the midlife transition when he attempts to re-appraise his life. (Levinson et al., 1978, pp. 153–154)

Meanwhile, a "keeping up with the Joneses" variety of competitiveness can burden the young adult's ago. Dormant sibling rivalries can raise their ugly heads and contribute to envy and greed; making money and purchasing things then becomes a pursuit in itself rather than being a conduit to domestic tranquility. Induction of "false needs" (Akhtar, 2014b), a tactic that forms the core of a consumer-driven economy, and the linkage of personal success with financial worth, a measure that is rampant in capitalistic societies, add fuel to the fire of passionate acquisitiveness. This is the negative dimension of *Grahastha* or the householder phase of a young adult's life.

Enjoying love, sex, and marriage

The greater synthesis of affection and lust and the subsequent birth of the capacity for mature love (Freud, 1912d) toward the end of adolescence prepares the young adult for serious, committed relationships. Dating ceases to be frivolous and a conscious or preconscious search for a life partner appears on the horizon. At this point, the young adult has to painstakingly work through his or her "ideal spouse representation" (Colarusso, 1997); this refers to the image of a future husband or wife that is evolved during adolescence and is heavily influenced by infantile omnipotence and oedipal strivings. Mourning over the loss of this intrapsychic structure is painful and takes place only over a protracted period of time. The young adult slowly comes to accept that "Mr. Right," or "Ms Right," are products of fantasy, and "Mr. Right-enough" and

"Ms Right-enough" are, in the end, more realistic and mature choices. This, by no means, implies the death of romantic love. In fact, the renunciation of infantile aims, synthesis of libido and aggression, and bringing together of affection and lust give birth to the capacity for real love (Bergmann, 1971; Kernberg, 1974a, 1974b) and enhance the depth of sensual pleasure in the context of mutuality.

Needless to add that arrival at this step is preceded by the need to decide whether one wishes to marry at all. That such decision warrants much intrapsychic work is illustrated by the rather unlikely source of the great Charles Darwin's (1809–1882) personal diary. Writing about this developmental step, the great scientist highlights his view of the key advantages and disadvantages of marriage:

> This is the Question
> *Not Marry*
> Freedom to go where one liked—choice of society and little of it. Conversation of clever men at clubs. Not forced to visit relatives and to bend in every trifle—to have the expense and anxiety of children—perhaps quarrelling—loss of time .... How should I manage all my business if I were obliged to go every day walking with my wife. Ehu! I should never know French, or see the Continent, or go to America, or go up in a Balloon.
> *Marry*
> Children (if it please God), constant companion (and friend in old age) who will feel interested in one .... My God, it is intolerable to think of spending one's whole life, like a neuter bee, working, working, and nothing after all. No, no, won't do. Imagine living all one's day solitarily in smoky dirty London house. Only picture to yourself a nice soft wife on a sofa with good fire, & books, & music perhaps .... Marry—Marry—Marry. (Darwin, 1838, p. 3)

Darwin's musings are exceptional in their insight, fair-mindedness, and, ultimately, their leading to a satisfactory resolution. While some of these issues are addressed premaritally, many others are actually solved in the early phases of marriage. This is the period with the greatest challenges to the partners' capacity for resilience. That such psychological burden occurs in the setting of increased romance and erotic excitement can have a dual effect. On the one hand, it can make the emotional challenges more bearable than these would otherwise be. On the other hand, the erotic excitement can detract from deeper psychological tasks while also making the partners more raw emotionally, thus interfering with their ability to peacefully negotiate their way out of conflicts and divergences.

Entry into marriage brings its own challenges. Broadly speaking, these can be divided into two categories: (i) intrapsychic, and (ii) interpersonal. The first and foremost intrapsychic task pertains to a thorough reworking of the remnant psychic splits involving affection and sex, as well as those involving love and aggression. The former, though mostly under control by the end of adolescence and later, entry into marriage, nonetheless demand revisiting. A spouse is a "relative" and thus, in the deepest layers of the wishful unconscious, stands in proximity with the "relatives" of early childhood, namely parents and siblings. This primary process overlap can stimulate oedipal longings and fears. These, in turn, require containment with grace, tolerance, and humor within the couple's relationship. Sexual prowess is at its peak during this time. Men have steel-hard erections. Women's breasts defy gravity. Erotic desire arises frequently and spontaneously. According to large population surveys (Hite, 1976, 1981; Kinsey et al., 1948, 1953; Masters & Johnson, 1966, 1970), couples under thirty have sexual intercourse 112 times a year on average. But this frequency declines to 86 times a year among thirty to thirty-nine year olds and 69 times a year for those ages forty to forty-nine. Late twenties and early thirties are the most active sexual periods for both men and women, though there is some suggestion that men's sexuality peaks earlier than that of women who become more sexually comfortable in their late thirties. However, as both men and women approach their late forties, the frequency of sexual intercourse declines. This requires emotional acceptance and adaptation without shame and anxiety.

Another intrapsychic issue is that of tolerating increased separation from the respective families of origin. One can no longer run to mother and father for "advice." Instead, one must rely upon the spouse who, being of approximately the same age group, might not evoke such anaclitic trust. Nonetheless, a shift of this sort has to be made in order to avoid causing narcissistic injury to the partner. Increasing distance from parents is, however, compensated by an intensifying role-related identification with them. Thus, a young man who has taken on the husband role now begins to have a deeper empathy with his father's position as a husband. Similarly in a new marriage, the young wife begins to sense what it might have been (and is) for her mother to be a wife. In this context, Balsam's (2000) concept of "mother within the mother" finds a parallel, naming the "wife within the wife." Such firming up of post-oedipal organization gives the self a rich and mature texture. However, this is not the only source of changes in identity during this period.

> Alteration in identity also results from the renunciation of potential objects of erotic desire and the corresponding self-representations, however imaginary the latter might be. Commitment to one's spouse—regardless of a name change—itself leads to incorporation of new internal objects, which, in turn, has a transformative impact upon one's identity. Additionally, in new marriage, the partners pick up verbal and non-verbal expressions from each other, and this alters their idiom of life in subtle but important ways. Such psychic alterations are neither conflict-free nor devoid of a sense of loss. However, through a gradual mourning process, in the setting of a loving relationship, the changed identity becomes not only bearable but, in the end, a source of pleasure. (Akhtar & Billinkoff, 2011, p. 117)

On the interpersonal front, there is the inevitable overlapping of identities of the two partners. Neither can remain entirely unchanged. Some relaxation of the boundaries of the self is essential in order to evolve marital mutuality; the concepts of "we-go" (G. Klein, 1967) as against "ego," "we-ness" (Bergman, 1980), and "we-self" (Roland, 1996), although proposed in contexts other than marriage, address this very type of functionally useful, merged states of the ego. However, this does not mean a total surrender of one's authenticity and separateness. Ideally, the partners retain main aspects of their private selves while renouncing some autonomy and also gradually taking in the internal objects of the partner.

Such developments test the capacity of marital partners to maintain "optimal distance" (Akhtar, 1992; Escoll, 1992; Mahler et al., 1975) as well as "optimal closeness" (Edward et al., 1981) within their relationship. An area rife with challenges for resilience and flexibility, this distance–closeness negotiation can, at times, result in chronic marital maladjustment. Like Schopenhauer's (1851) porcupines, such partners fluctuate between intimacy and distance, trust and mistrust, betrayal and confession, and separation and reunion. They cannot live peacefully together, nor can they do without each other. They lack the capacity to establish complementarity of roles and are unable to follow Khalil Gibran's (1883–1931) counsel for marital partners to:

> … stand together yet not too near together:
> For the pillars of the temple stand apart, and the oak tree and the cypress grow
> not in each other's shadow. (1923, p. 16)

Although the proximity afforded by marriage does play a triggering role, such hopeless failure in negotiating an optimal distance often betrays separate character pathology in the two partners.

Difficulties also arise in the encounter with in-laws. Partners in marriage have to learn to know and get along, if not like, their "new relatives." The relational matrix in which a positive or negative emotional bond with parents-in-law has to evolve is far from simple. It involves (i) internal comparison of spouse's parents with one's own parents, (ii) rivalry for attention from the spouse who has an inevitable internal and external dialogue of greater force and continuity with one's in-laws, (iii) regressive longings (and defenses against them) for parental love from in-laws and the attendant rivalry with the spouse for their attention, and (iv) competitive strivings (with all their sublime and overt hostile dimensions) with the parent-in-law of the opposite sex in a modified enactment of the oedipal scenario. Working in unison, such meta-dynamics of the in-law relationships can tax the newlywed's ego. Additional complications can arise from the involvement with brothers- and sisters-in-law. Interacting with them can bring forth unresolved issues of sibling rivalry, sibling envy, and even "sibling hunger." Depending upon the actual configuration of siblings in the two families (e.g., one having only brothers, the other only sisters), the outcome can be highly varied. In the end though, what matters is whether libido or aggression is the dominant force in the marital psychic economy and how resilient the two partners are themselves. To be sure, empathy, understanding, and lack of hurry and pressure in evolving a relationship can be quite helpful, especially if these are coming not only from the spouse, but also from the in-laws themselves.

Becoming a parent and partaking of its attendant responsibilities and pleasures

It is generally agreed upon that parenthood consists of four stages: (i) an anticipatory stage that begins in childhood and lasts till pregnancy, (ii) a "honeymoon" stage that lasts from the child's birth till he or she becomes five to six months old;[32] (iii) a plateau stage from the offspring's infancy to adolescence, and (iv) a "letting go" or disengagement state which begins in the child's adolescence and culminates in his or her marriage (GAP Report, cited in Parens, 1975). The first of these four stages, especially the desire to become a parent, was the topic of a seminal contribution by Benedek (1959). Introducing the term "primary reproductive drive" (p. 394) and staying loyal to the classical psychosexual theory, Benedek proposed that:

> The mother's object relationship with the child is motivated by psychic energies originating in two levels of her psychosexual organization. One is the primary reproductive drive, the other is a secondary organization, derived from the oral phase of her development. The first is manifested by the adult tendency to give, to nurse, tend to succor; the other by manifestation of receptive tendencies. This facilitates the mother's identification with her child. (p. 394)

Of note here is Benedek's bold departure from Freud's (1925j) proposal that the girl's desire to have a baby is a way of consoling herself for the

---

[32] Winnicott's (1956a) phase of "primary maternal preoccupation" corresponds to this period. During it, the mother loses interest in her "other-than-mother" identities (e.g., wife, sister, daughter, professional worker) and gives herself completely over to her role as an infant's mother.

absence of a penis: "If I cannot have a penis, at least I can have my father's penis, and through it, his baby."

Turning her attention to the father, Benedek retained the same two-tier model, though, in my reading of it, this was accomplished by her in a somewhat contorted devotion to the instinct theory. According to her, there are "two sources of fatherhood: one biological bisexuality, and the other biological dependency upon the mother and consequent maternal identifications" (p. 397) which are lived out as "identifications" (p. 397) with the wife during pregnancy. Benedek also attributed a greater societal pressure on men to beget progeny, a proposal that actually might apply more to women.[33]

Another early contributor to the parenthood literature was Kestenberg (cited in Parens, 1975), who also paid greater attention to the origins of the desire to be a parent rather than the consequences.[34] She did, however, note that fathers, as a rule, show more aggression toward their offspring than do mothers. Paternal aggression appears after a short period of tenderness and is expressed in exuberant motor playfulness that often camouflages unconscious fantasies of castration and murder. Kestenberg emphasized that a change in the psychic structure of the parent invariably occurs whenever a successful subphase of parenthood is completed.

It is such consequences of becoming a parent that matter most in our discussion of adult development. And here, the work of Erikson (1950b, 1959), Lidz (1968), Colarusso (1990), Stern (1995), and Balsam

---

[33] That evolutionary forces also contribute to the drive to produce offspring goes without saying. This theme, along with its corollary of the mate-selection process, is thoroughly elaborated upon by Baselice and Thomson (2018).

[34] Ross (1977) has painstakingly traced the gradual development and consolidation of the "paternal identity" in boys. He suggests that such development undergoes six phases: (i) identification with the caregiving functions of the mother; (ii) a "hermaphroditic" phase where the boy imagines having both a penis and inner reproductive spaces like his mother, (iii) with the onset of the phallic phase, the evolution of an image of a giving, productive father, (iv) realizing that he is still a child and feeling frustrated at not being able to become a father right away, a turning away to work and learning from mentors, (v) arriving at "his hard-won generational authority and newfound responsibility as a procreator, a producer, and a caretaker to his own children" (p. 345), and finally (vi) being en route to a "paternity of self" (Erikson, 1950b).

(2000) captures our attention. In his detailed, psychosocial task-oriented deconstruction of the human life span, Erikson (1950b) emphasized that the emergence of "generativity" is a crucial feature of mature adult development. According to him,

> Generativity is primarily the concern in establishing and guiding the next generation, although there are individuals who, through misfortune or because of special and genuine gifts in other directions, do not apply this drive to their own offspring. And, indeed, the concept of generativity is meant to include such popular synonyms as *productivity*, and *creativity*, which however cannot replace it. (p. 267, italics in the original)

Erikson emphasized that merely having children does not mobilize generativity[35] and in certain narcissistic individuals, parenthood actually retards its development. His notion of generativity, though limited in its application to parenthood per se, was actually given depth and texture by subsequent contributors. Lidz (1968) emphasized that becoming a parent has deep and wide-ranging effects upon the individual, his or her relationship with the partner, and the couple's position in society. While the infant represents a physical fusion of the parents and becomes a lifelong bond between them, the impact upon the mother and father shows significant differences.

> The birth of a child turns a wife into a woman by setting her on a par with her mother. Her love for the husband who has made such completion possible deepens. She does not wish the child just for herself but as meaningful outcome of her relatedness to her husband, pleasing him with a gift that is something of him that he has placed in her to nurture but also something of herself that the husband will cherish. To some extent, the baby is herself loved by a benevolent father. The process carries residue of the

---

[35] In an empirical study of young parents, Slater (2015) confirmed that parenthood and generativity are not inextricably linked. And coming from the opposite direction, Quinodoz (2010) emphasized that "Even a woman without children of her own may have developed the maternal side of her femininity" (p. 90) and thus be quite generative.

> little girl's envy of the mother who could produce a child with and for the father. (p. 471)

And, for the new father, Lidz (1968) said the following:

> Paradoxically, even as paternity secures and heightens a father's masculine self-esteem and permits realization of his instrumental functions of protecting and providing, it also affords him with an opportunity to express the nurturant qualities derived from his early identification with his mother that previously had few acceptable outlets and required repression. The child's admiration and adulation of him will provide him with narcissistic supplies, and he now gains the position and status of "father" that he had envied and desired to attain since his earliest childhood. There are also forces that promote jealousy of a child, and antagonisms to a child, particularly a son, that are held before us in myth. The husband may resent his wife's attention to the child, and old sibling rivalries may thus be rekindled. (p. 472)

Such father–child nexus of hostile competitiveness has been a theme of global folklore and myth;[36] an elaboration of it is to be found in Ross' (1994) description of the "Laius complex," which is a hostile counterpart to the male child's Oedipus complex. Bergman (2004), however, emphasized that in order to fully embrace fatherhood, it is not sufficient to master one's oedipal struggles. In her opinion, an exhaustive working-through of "the earliest relationship with the mother contributes a great deal to the emotional quality of the father's relationship to his baby" (p. 126). While mostly agreeing with Bergman, Blum (2004) wondered if her proposal "in a sexist fashion, suggests that nurturance is inherently the province of the female and maternal, and not of the male and paternal?" (p. 140). He also noted that the baby can become a significant

---

[36] Greek mythology is especially replete with tales of violence and warfare between fathers and sons. Kronos, for instance, castrated his father, Ouranos, and Tantalus (a son of Zeus) killed his son Pelops, boiled him, and served him up in a banquet for the gods (Houtzager, 2004).

transference object for the father. All in all, the psychoanalytic views on the effects of becoming a father have grown more textured and nuanced.

Advances have also been made in our understanding of maternal psychology. Winnicott's (1956a) "primary maternal preoccupation," mentioned earlier in this chapter, laid the groundwork for many later contributions of significance. Two outstanding ones are (i) Stern's (1995) concept of the "motherhood constellation," a psychic state that brings forth "the mother's discourse with her own mother-as-mother-to-her-as-a-child; her discussion with herself, especially with herself as a mother; and her discourse with her baby" (p. 174), and (ii) Balsam's (2000) concept of the "mother-within-the-mother" which proposes that the inner dialogue a woman has with her mother does not begin with pregnancy, as Stern proposed, but represents the "psychodynamic development of a continuous inner evolution of [the] mother-daughter relationship" (p. 484).

The pervasive impact of parenthood on the emotional life of young adults was, however, elaborated in the greatest detail by Colarusso (1990, 1995; Colarusso & Nemiroff, 1981). He referred to the identity transformations consequent upon parenthood as a "third individuation"[37] and declared that this constitutes:

> … a situation in which infantile themes and relationships can be reworked in relation to phase-specific, adult, developmental tasks and conflicts. For example, by becoming involved parents, adults attempt to replicate the profoundly gratifying childhood experience of intimacy with their own infantile objects, which leads to the realization that their bodies and minds, their sense of self, emanated exclusively from the man and woman who had created and raised them. Further, becoming parents allows them to play

[37] The term "third individuation" has a curious history in psychoanalysis. It was introduced by Oldham (1989) in describing the effect of parental aging and death upon their adult offspring. Then it was used by Colarusso (1990) to describe the impact of parenthood on young adults. And, finally, with no knowledge of these earlier usages, I employed the term to designate the restructuring of identity following immigration (Akhtar, 1995).

> the active and dominant role in a parent–child relationship, facilitating a reworking of old infantile feelings of passivity and submission. Then, as their own child gradually assumes parental powers and prerogatives, the parents are forced to temper aspects of their own residual infantile narcissism and omnipotence. (Colarusso, 1990, p. 184)

Colarusso noted that each phase of the offspring's psychic development affects the emotional equilibrium of the parents. Giving birth to a child deepens the sense of parental masculinity and femininity, enhances their narcissism, and mobilizes fresh capacities for concern and generosity. Aggressive instincts are also mobilized, especially with the child's entry into the anal phase and his or her increasing willfulness. Parents' own separation–individuation experiences get activated, even if on an unconscious level, and impact upon their responses to the child's locomotion, negativism, and self-assertion. As this is going on, a new sense of parity with one's own parents emerges. Comparisons are constantly made with how one is raising the child and how one was raised; this has the potential of increasing both the loving and hateful feelings toward one's parents. Matters are made more complex as the child enters the oedipal phase. Parental love now acquires a sexual, even though subtle, dimension.

> Old childhood wishes for access to and control of their own parent's body, particularly the genitals, are gratified through access to the infant's and child's body, i.e., changing diapers and bathing. More direct sexual wishes are gratified by taking oedipal-aged children into bed, showering with them, exposing them to the primal scene, or by responding to their seductive behavior.
>
> A new healthy dimension is added to the new parents' sexuality when these feelings are engaged and mastered. By tolerating the seductiveness of an immature being who is a biological extension of themselves, and by controlling their own responses so as not to interact with the child inappropriately, parents achieve additional mastery of infantile sexual impulses and experiences

> and a new sense of separateness from infantile introjects. (Colarusso, 1990, p. 190)[38]

Colarusso also highlighted the fact that playing with latency-age children and teaching them new reality-oriented skills, while also letting the children "keep" the accomplishments as their own, strengthens the parental identity. The adolescence of one's children puts such identity to its more severe test, not only because the child is trying to disengage and create his or her own identity but also because the erotic and aggressive components of the Oedipus complex are re-triggered with considerable ferocity. Loewald (1979) reminds us that not only "in adolescence the Oedipus rears its head again [but] so it does during later periods in life, in normal people as well as in neurotics" (p. 753). As a result, parents need to work through their sexual curiosities and hostile rivalries toward their children at this step.

While Colarusso deserves credit for providing the most comprehensive summary of such developments, the fact is that earlier analysts had also addressed these matters, albeit in a piecemeal fashion. Winnicott (1960a) emphasized that the child's move from absolute dependence to relative dependence "takes place *because of the baby's experience of the mother's* (or mother substitute's) *adaptive behavior*" (p. 247, italics in the original). Mahler (1970) noted that the child's striving toward separation mobilizes affects in the mother that she must confront and master again and again; a mother's unique response will depend upon her own early experiences of separation which now have to be reworked. Anthony (1970) delineated parental responses to the oedipal phase of the child, noting that the "degree to which the oedipal conflict is still unresolved in the parent will influence the Oedipus complex in the child in the direction of non-resolution" (p. 286). Kestenberg (1975) highlighted the enhancement of epistemic and playful character traits in parents by the entry of their children in the latency phase, and Blos (1967, 1985) observed that in bearing the anxieties caused by adolescent children's rebellious dis-identifications, parents mellow and gradually replace their

---

[38] See in this context, my concept of the "civilizing influence of the daughter" (2009a, p. 47).

sense of omnipotence with an awareness of the limits of their control over their children.

Such modal reverberations have acquired new hues with the "changing mythology of parenthood" (Parens, 2016). Thus, the joys and challenges faced by mothers who are single (O'Neil, 2016), recently immigrants (Akhtar, 1999a, 2011a; Y. Harrison, 2016; Tummala-Narra, 2004), and lesbian (Frank, 2016; Glazer, 2016) and fathers who are gay (Glazer & Drescher, 2001) might have important similarities and differences with those faced by heterosexual parents in "traditional" households.[39]

Not only is there a great variability in the intra-familial experiences of parenthood, the arrival of a child also causes significant shifts in relationships with the spouse and the society at large. Within the marital relationship, the entry of a "third party" can play emotional havoc (with the mobilization of jealousy, rivalry, etc.) or it can act as a libidinal glue (with the deepening of mutuality, shared enjoyment of parental roles). On the one hand, "Ethnic or social class difference in role expectations which had been inconsequential in the marital relationships can become more troublesome when they concern child-rearing practices (Lidz, 1968, p. 347). On the other hand, the marital bond may find a new vigor with there now being a further source of common interest and joint identification. Dynamic shifts are also evident in the couple's relationship to the society at large. New sets of relationships are sought and established as parents are drawn to the other couples with children of the same age. As the child grows, babysitters, kindergarten teachers, parent–teacher associations, summer camp organizers, and, of course, one's parents and parents-in-law become more and more part of the couple's growing family. As children traverse adolescence and begin to dream about their "grown-up lives", time suddenly announces its passing in louder tones. One is now arriving in an entirely new phase of life, it says.

---

[39] In addition to these variables, there is the whole separate and complex realm of adoptive parenthood, with a voluminous literature of its own (e.g. Akhtar & Kramer, 1999; Frank, 2016; Winzinger et al., 2016).

Midlife

Generally speaking, the time period between forty-five and sixty years or so is referred to as "midlife."[40] With young adulthood behind one, and old age still distant, midlife is a period of further psychic maturation as well as that of much emotional turmoil. Four major tasks of this developmental era include: (i) noticing and accepting changes in one's body and their impact upon identity, (ii) encountering limits in diverse psychosocial realms, (iii) accommodating to changes in the relationships with one's parents, and (iv) letting go of children. Comments on each of these issues follow.

Noticing and accepting changes in one's body and their impact upon identity

Changes in one's body and its functioning become unmistakably evident during midlife. The most common among these are changes in vision, joint flexibility, and fat distribution (Lachman, 2004). With growing age, the lens of the eye gets larger but the eye loses some of its flexibility to adjust to visual stimuli. Night vision especially begins to suffer. Joint flexibility diminishes and occasional aches and pains become a feature of life. Accumulation of fat in the abdomen leads to weight gain; this tendency is also fueled by the slowing down of metabolism in this age. Hearing loss is experienced by some 14 percent of midlife adults (Armstrong et al., 2019). Changes also become evident in sexual life. Reaching their fifties, men begin to have less-hard erections. Women undergo menopause; their vaginal walls thin and lubrication with sexual receptivity becomes less generous. The frequency of sexual intercourse within the couple diminishes (Hite, 1976, 1981; Kinsey et al., 1948, 1953; Masters & Johnson, 1966, 1970). Physical attractiveness might be affected in both sexes by the appearance of wrinkles and lessening of sheen in the skin. Men might begin to develop baldness and women's

---

[40] As stated earlier in this chapter, such age limits are not strict. Sociocultural features and the average life expectancy of a given era or geographical region can easily shift them in one or the other direction. Jaques (1965), for instance, placed the onset of middle age at thirty-seven years.

breasts sag. And, both men and women might show a diminution in the speed of cognitive data processing (Lachman, 2004). Changes in sleep patterns also become noticeable with advancing age.

The emotional impact of such bodily changes varies greatly. One not infrequent reaction is "a continuous, conscious and unconscious, narcissistically injurious comparison of the midlife body with the body of young adulthood" (Colarusso, 1997, p. 81). Breakdown of hope, depression, and cynicism accompanying such a state can cause self-neglect and lead one to giving up hitherto passionately held vocational goals and hobbies. Or, "manic defense" (Klein, 1935) can come into play resulting in frenetic overactivity and grotesque attempts at recapturing youthful appearance and physical rejuvenation of unrealistic proportions. The latter outcome is often associated with the dissolution of a long-term marriage, extramarital affairs, and geographic relocation that surprises all friends and acquaintances; this constitutes a true "midlife crisis" (Jaques, 1965) in colloquial parlance.[41] Such "depressive" and "manic" outcomes are more frequent in individuals with excessive amounts of narcissism (Kernberg, 1980).

In relatively balanced persons, there emerges a gradual adaptation to the changed body image. On the materialistic front, the polarities of asceticism and greed find a synthesis, with acquisition becoming less and pleasure in what one has becoming more intense. Such people face midlife bodily changes with relative equanimity and undertake more realistic attempts at adaptation. Their attempts to cope are mostly "autoplastic" (Hartmann, 1939) in nature. Changes in diet, reading glasses, and above all, ongoing or newly instituted regimens of physical exercise come to one's rescue. The use of dietary supplements and low-dose hormonal support (testosterone for men, estrogen for women) might also be helpful.

All in all, the emotional consequences of the inevitable physical changes during midlife seem to depend upon the preexisting (i) dominance of narcissism in the individual's life; (ii) degree of psychic fragility vis-à-vis the bodily strength and body image and, (iii) extent of

[41] Midlife leads to a diminution of sexual promiscuity in hitherto outgoing and boastful narcissistic individuals (Kernberg, 1980) but can unleash the emergence of sexual excess and even perversions in the "shy narcissists" (Akhtar, 2000).

masochistically driven "love" for self-dissipation in the economy of his or her internal world. Those who are pathologically narcissistic, shaky in their somatic confidence, and/or masochistically idealizing of decay do not do well with aging. Those who are deeply object-related, bodily secure, and appropriately self-protective can bear the storm of midlife changes with relative equanimity.

One less commented upon change, discernible even in the well-adjusted group, is a shift in the inherently bisexual configuration of the core identity. This transformation was first commented upon by Jung (1933) who wrote:

> We might compare masculinity and femininity to a particular store of substances of which, in the first half of life, unequal use is made. A man consumes his large supply of masculine substance, and has left over only the smaller amount of feminine substance, which he must now put to use. It is the other way around with a woman: she allows her unused supply of masculinity to become more active. (p. 107)

Jung's "energic" and slightly mysterious speculations found empirical support in Vaillant's (1977) long-term follow-up study of "normal" adult men and women who were gradually advancing in age.

> As they grow older, women grow facial hair, and men's beards grow more slowly. Women become flat-chested, their voices deepen; their facial features sharpen, and the estrogens that may inhibit dominance decrease. The breasts of old men grow, their faces soften, and the androgenic hormones facilitating dominance decrease. Perhaps older women may frighten younger men because they have grown more comfortable with assertive impulses. Perhaps older men may appeal to younger women precisely because they can let themselves become more gentle and nurturant. (p. 234)

Such changes in the intrapsychic gender configuration and the associated reformulation of identity and attitudes have also been noted by Gutmann (1980): "The postparental period gives back to women their covert masculinity, to men their covert femininity; thus, each parent recaptures some of the self-potentials that they had parceled out to the mate, and both retrieve some quotient of the narcissism that they had conceded to their offspring" (p. 80).

Such narcissistic expansion, however, does not preclude the quietly perceived narrowing of life in many other realms.

Encountering limits in diverse psychosocial realms

As the individual arrives at the threshold of midlife, he begins to sense that there are limits to what he can achieve or do in this world. The allure of material acquisitions that he fervently pursued during his youth now begins to wane. More can no longer be acquired, or can only be acquired at a huge loss on some other front; it therefore seems less appealing. In the intellectual and creative realms, too, one begins to notice the limits of one's vision and capability. Wishful self-representations, which one thought would be realized "someday" (Akhtar, 1996), reveal their illusory nature. The physician who held the fantasy of acquiring a law degree in the future now finds that he has to let go of that idea. The schoolteacher who always wanted to enter active politics but kept postponing it realizes during middle or late middle age that it is too late to get on a party bandwagon. Such an encounter with life's limits often leaves one stunned. A desire to question and modify the life's course now arises and this may not be entirely pathological. Allow me to quote Levinson et al. (1978) at some length here.

> The doubting and searching are appropriate to this period; the real question is how best to make use of them. The problem is compounded by the fact that the process of re-appraisal activates unconscious conflicts—the unconscious baggage carried forward from hard times in the past which hinders the effort to change. The pathology is not in the desire to improve one's life but in the obstacles to pursuing the same .... A profound reappraisal of this kind cannot be a cool, intellectual process. It must involve emotional turmoil, despair, the sense of not knowing where to turn or of being stagnant and unable to move at all. A man in this state often makes false starts. He tentatively tests a variety of new

> choices, not only out of confusion or impulsiveness but, equally, out of a need to explore, to see what is possible, to find out how it feels to engage in a particular love relationship, occupation, or solitary pursuit. Every genuine reappraisal must be agonizing, because it challenges the illusions and vested interests on which the existing structure is based. (p. 199)

One's sense of the passage of time is also affected. Months and years seem to fly by. One can no longer multiply one's age by two and remain convinced that one would still be alive. Consequently, one concludes that more of one's life is behind and less is left to live. Middle age thus causes an uncanny shift in the individual's perspective of time. The inherent transience[42] of all relationships becomes undeniable.

> Even the stability of the inanimate world now seems threatened: the cities one knows from the past change, neighborhoods change, and these external changes may symbolize and reinforce all mourning processes regarding loss and separation. The awareness of the ephemerality of human life becomes a very concrete force which increases mourning processes—and growth connected with them—and fosters an orientation to both the past that is gone and the future that now seems nearer ... To accept oneself within such limits is an important aspect of emotional maturity that is in contrast to narcissistic rationalization, to denial, to resignation and cynicism, and masochistic self-blame. (Kernberg, 1980, pp. 126–127)

The encounter with limits that happens during middle age is eloquently captured in the poem, *Limits*, by the renowned Argentinian poet, Jorge Luis Borges (1899–1986).

> There is a line by Verlaine that I will not remember again.
> There is a street nearby that is off-limits to my feet.

---

[42] The mere fact that something, some relationship, some experience, or even life as a whole, is transient does not have to rob one's capacity to enjoy it. In fact, transience can paradoxically enhance the value of an experience (Freud, 1916a).

There is a mirror that has seen me for the last time.
There is a door I have closed until the end of the world.
Among the books in my library (I'm looking at them now)
  are some I will never open.
This summer I will be fifty years old.
Death is using me up, relentlessly. (1964, p. 139)

Middle age thus brutally diminishes one's omnipotence and makes one aware of the reduced sense of the time allotted for one to live. Such sharpened awareness of the passage of time impacts the work of creative people in three different ways (Jaques, 1965): "The creative career may simply come to an end, either in a drying up of creative work, or in actual death; the creative capacity may begin to show and express itself for the first time; or a decisive change in the quality and content of creativeness may take place" (p. 502). Extending this last point, Jaques proposed that during midlife, the "intense and spontaneous" (p. 502) creativity changes into "sculpted creativity [where there is] a big step between the first effusion of inspiration and the finished creative product" (p. 503).

Intellectual shifts do not exhaust the list of stressful changes during midlife. The external markers of accumulated wealth, material possessions, and educational qualifications also undergo a change, often coming to a gradual halt. There is not much further one can go. One begins to have a sense of the finiteness of one's possessions, possibilities, and power. Paradoxically, at this very juncture dawns the awareness that one's parents are fading and need to be taken care of.

Accommodating to the changed relationship with one's parents

As one enters the forties to fifties, one's parents turn seventy to eighty years old. Their health begins to be compromised and their capability to live autonomously gradually becomes questionable. They require frequent visits to doctors' offices and find the necessary chores of daily life (e.g., grocery shopping) difficult to negotiate. It is at this point that the middle-aged individual has to step in and provide them assistance. Besides the real encroachment on time and physical resources, this reversal of the parent–child relationship (whereby the parent becomes the dependent one) has the potential to stir up earlier, unresolved conflicts that have been "deferred" in their full expression as well as new conflicts which are contemporary and consciously experienced.

Collectively, these conflicts subsume four psychosocial realms: (i) denial vs. acceptance of parental frailty, (ii) triumphant vs. tender attitude toward parents, (iii) loyalty conflicts between the family of origin vs. the post-marital family of one's own, and (iv) secrecy vs. openness and balancing the psychic accounts. The *first* matter involves experiencing, bearing, and managing the powerful emotions mobilized by seeing one's parents as weak and fallible. Realistic perception demands acceptance but infantile emotions propel denial. Repeated confrontations with reality, often in the form of advice given by parents' physicians, helps the metabolism of the difficult emotions involved on a preconscious level. The *second* matter follows such acceptance and pertains to how one feels toward one's parents that one can see as physically and psychosocially vulnerable. Whether one reacts with hostility, contempt, triumphant mockery, and pity, or responds with enhanced tenderness and compassion depends upon how well resolved were earlier separateness-related and oedipal conflicts. Becoming increasingly absorbed in the care of aging parents can, however, be the result of both such new-found affection and a reaction formation against emergent hostility. Either scenario can stir up the *third* issue mentioned above. This pertains to the conflicts of loyalty between paying attention to one's parents and paying attention to one's spouse and children. Daughters and daughters-in-law typically get readily pulled into such tugs of war, though sons and sons-in-law are hardly immune to be torn along these lines. Such conflicts often put strain on the marital bond and require much empathy and consideration from the spouse. The *fourth* and final issue pertains to family secrets. As parents age, they might reveal long-held secrets[43] in the hope of balancing the relational books, so to speak, before departing from this world. Such secrets are mostly minor, though, at times, can pertain to serious and shocking matters (e.g., who is the real father of whom, did that uncle really die of tuberculosis or had he taken his own life?).

---

[43] For a deeper psychological understanding of secrets and secret-keeping, see Margolis (1966, 1974) and Khan (1983a, 1983b).

As such things are worked out, more time passes. Parents become truly infirm and often need to be placed in nursing homes and even under hospice care. And, then comes the end of their lives. The death of parents almost always has a profound effect on the surviving middle-aged offspring. Though it is not entirely clear, there does seem to be some difference in the way adults react to the death of their mothers and their fathers. Mother's death which, according to Freud, mobilizes "emotions that are hard to grasp" (letter to Max Eitingon, December 1, 1929, cited in Eissler, 1976, p. 233) has the potential of destabilizing the core holding object. Father's death, in contrast, tends to stir up hitherto dormant parricidal wishes and can become a source of guilt. There might also exist differences in the way men and women react to their parents' death. Men might experience greater difficulty reconciling with their deceased but internally alive father (Wolman, 2017). Women might respond to their father's death with dynamic shifts, and to their mother's death by structural alterations (Meyers, 2001); in them, identification with the deceased mother seems greater than that with the deceased father. Masur (2001) disagrees with this view and suggests that such identification often has strong defensive functions.[44]

Regardless of whether it is mother's or father's, the death of parents robs one of the last vestiges of infantile omnipotence whereby one felt somehow protected from death oneself. It is as if the parents, regardless of their age and fragility, acted as an umbrella, the loss of which leaves one exposed. Now it is one's turn in the "succession" to mortality. The existential loneliness of this phase is often compounded by the changing relationship with one's children.

Letting go of the children

The middle-aged individual faces increasing psychological separation from his or her children as they take their first steps on the path to adulthood. Most middle- and upper-class parents watch their children leave to start college. In the words of Coburn and Treeger (1997),

---

[44] Schlesinger (2003), Singletary (2001), and Vahip (2019) have highlighted the necessary adjustments of psychoanalytic technique when an adult analysand loses a parent during the course of treatment.

> The prelude to the actual countdown starts with a familiar invasion of the mailbox—no longer overstuffed with shiny new books as it had been last year, but now carrying a steady stream of letters about housing options, campus organizations, and course selections, all with the same increasingly familiar college logo—a relentless reminder of the fall to come. (p. 113)

And the exciting and yet vaguely dreaded fall does arrive. Parents help pack what their child is to take along with him or her to college. With this comes the first pang of realization that something intangible yet powerful is coming to an end. The child's room—so "homey" with its familiar accoutrements—begins to appear different as things from it make their way into packed duffel bags. His or her rush (developmentally appropriate and/or defensive) for parents to leave and to be alone once all the stuff makes its way to the college campus is yet another reminder of an era having ended. Parents come back to a changed home that despite being quiet does not feel peaceful. There is sadness in the air.

The subsequent period of mourning and adaptation is made easier by the fact that there remains an emotional and financial "tether" (Akhtar, 1992), which periodically pulls the child back for refueling. Such visits have a rhythmic quality to them and occur around major holidays (e.g., Thanksgiving, Christmas) and breaks in the academic schedule. The returning "child," however, treats the home as a hotel. He spends more time outside the house socializing with his "local" friends than at home relating to his family. Nonetheless, his home visits have the potential of kindling earlier affects and creating an illusory sense that "the good old days" when the parents and child lived together on a daily basis have come back.

This changes dramatically when children—now actually, young adults—find love, cohabit with their partners, become engaged and get married. The contrast (and, under unfortunate circumstances, conflict and clash) between the parental vision of the required rituals (most importantly, the wedding ceremony) and the young adult's own plans can become a painful reminder that one has to "let go" of the erstwhile authority and control over the latter. The addition of a son- or daughter-in-law to the family further alters the texture of its dialogue. New relational nuances appear. Parents can now reveal old secrets and even the complaints that they had held against their children since the latter have the support of their spouses and are better protected from narcissistic injury. However, new secrets develop as parents notice their offspring's relationship with their husbands and wives and feel that certain aspects of it are off-limits for discussion. In either case, the parent–child relationship is altered in deep and unchangeable ways. Children put a greater premium on their marital bond than on their filial ties. Their orbit shifts away from their parents. This becomes even more painfully evident as they begin families of their own. It is at this point that children "leave home" on a deeper level.

Living in an "empty nest," the middle-aged parents experience the need to reconfigure their relationships not only with their departed children (and their newly acquired sons- and daughters-in-law) but also, and more importantly, with each other. This last-mentioned avenue creates the possibility of deepened love between spouses, greater enjoyment of each other's company, with a sense of renewed freedom and discovery. Sadness at children's leaving home gives way to the enjoyment of "respite from parenthood" (Jane Brandt, personal communication, April 2015), greater liberty to travel, and more time to pick up on old interests and hobbies. This energic boost prepares one to enter the next and final phase of one's life.

Old age and death

This final phase of life is called "old age" and is customarily divided into "young old age" (65–80 years) and "old old age" (80 years and beyond). A period of profound biopsychosocial changes, old age can play havoc with one's emotions; the sardonic quip attributed to the Hollywood superstar of the 1940s and 1950s, Betty Davis (1908–1989), that "Old age ain't for sissies" captures the essence of the challenges an individual faces at this juncture of life. An attempt to describe the experience is also made in my following poems on aging.

Three poems on aging

I notice the direction of my toes change.
No textbook of geography had mentioned this.
But the one-eyed blacksmith of time knew it in advance.

* * *

I do not want to die but I have to.
So I better prepare myself, sort things out.
Make sure to not leave un-mailed letters in the drawers of my nightstand.
Put the garbage out.

* * *

I now think better on my feet while sitting in a chair.
My best thoughts will rise from a grave.

Three more poems on aging

I tell myself that conversation with them would be vacuous and boring,
When I see attractive women in their thirties.

* * *

I promise not to serve
more than six pancakes of platitude per week.

* * *

I find shoes with laces became a burden.
Who can tie all loose ends anyway?

Coda

I know men and women age differently,
are struck by different hammers of anatomy,
feel different shames.
But in death they become the same
Things.
(Akhtar, 2021, p. 47)

Let me not get ahead of myself, however. Allow me to return to the "scientific" tenor of this discourse on old age. In doing so, I am compelled to point out that this final phase of life has the major landmarks of (i) becoming a grandparent, (ii) downsizing and retiring from one's job, (iii) dealing with the deaths of friends, siblings, and spouses, and (iv) getting really old, facing infirmities, and preparing to die. To what extent these events are dealt with with feelings of equanimity, relief, and even joy[45] and how much anxiety, frustration, and sorrow they produce depends upon the preexisting economy of love and hate in one's inner world of self- and object relations as well as one's overall philosophy of life. A deeper look at each of these four landmark experiences sheds further light on what can and does happen in old age.

Becoming a grandparent and feeling rejuvenated by the experience

In the first ever psychoanalytic paper on grandparents, Abraham (1913) noted that "The special emphasis given to the grandfather or the grandmother was always rooted in a violent rejection of the father or the mother" (p. 44). While thus highlighting the pathological roots of the love of grandparents, Abraham also noted its developmentally useful role. Interaction with grandparents[46] demonstrates to the growing child that "Even the father on whom, by reason of his unconscious fixation, he feels wholly dependent, is not omnipotent, but is himself subject to a higher power" (p. 47). Abraham's focus in these comments, however, remained upon the grandchild's perspective and did not take into account the intrapsychic vicissitudes of grandparenthood in itself.

This was taken up by later investigators who declared grandparenthood to be one of life's sweetest pleasures (Cath, 1997; Colarusso, 1997). Although the name grandparents can, at time, feed into a naïve idealization of their role (Quinodoz, 2008), it also attests to the exalted

---

[45] In his remarkable book, *Tuesdays with Morrie*, the New York-based sports writer, Mitch Albom (1998) poignantly describes a series of visits with his former sociology professor, Morrie Schwartz, as the latter was becoming increasingly disabled and finally dying of ALS. Striking about the pieces contained in this book is the upbeat tone of Morrie's comments on his infirmity and approaching death.

[46] The significance of a child's relationship with his grandparents is especially evident in African American communities where the grandmother often plays a centrally organizing, near-paternal role in the former's development.

feeling associated with this developmental epoch. There are several reasons for grandparenthood being often more enjoyable than parenthood. To begin with, there is usually a diminution of aggressive drives such as envy and ambivalence that were present in the period of parenthood. Moreover, "By the time of becoming grandparents, the ego development has acquired much greater sophistication than was the case at the time of becoming parents. Acceptance of reality is deeper and the safe ego pleasures of life acquire a keener quality" (Kramer et al., 1997, p. 17). Consequently, people in the later periods of life are able to experience more pleasure and less pain than that experienced in parenthood. In addition, grandchildren provide grandparents with what Cath (1982) calls a "miracle of revitalization," whereby the grandparent gains a promise of the longevity of his line at a time when his own body begins to betray him. The same phenomenon is described from a slightly different vantage point by Colarusso (1997), who labeled it the "illusion of genetic immortality." He proposes that grandchildren offer a promise of defying death, as it were, through the continued life of future generations.

Colarusso (1997) adds that grandparents tend to idealize their grandchildren and shower them with intense love and admiration. Those with a greater capacity for self-observation and humor see though the falseness of such idealization while continuing to enjoy it. Others take the estimation of their grandchildren as factual. In either case, the idealization seems to serve many developmental and defensive purposes. Those include "(1) a narcissistic buffer against the stings of old age and the inevitability of death, (2) a chance for magical repair of one's own life through genetic immortality, and (3) a denial of unalterable imperfections in the self through selective identification with particular qualities in the grandchild" (pp. 90–91).

Together, these factors give rise to a sense of narcissistic gratification on the grandparents' part. The fact that the grandchild and the grandparent are united in their subtle (or not so subtle) resentment of the generation in between also enhances the grandparents' self-esteem. Grandchildren's use of the grandparents as some kind of "super-parents" also adds to the latter's narcissistic inflation (Abraham, 1913). Yet another source of happiness for grandparents is the fact that having grandchildren provides them with an opportunity to undo their remorse over their inadequacies as parents (Cath, 1982). All in all, being a grandparent is a source of great delight.

Downsizing and retiring from one's job

As one gets old, one's attitude toward material acquisition changes. One buys fewer and fewer things. One begins to think of unburdening oneself of the clutter of "things" around oneself. For those who have the affluence to consider such moves, a changeover to a smaller place of residence becomes attractive. The generosity that Klein (1957) had underscored as accompanying gratitude to life and the generativity that Erikson (1950b) had described as the sponsorship of the forthcoming generations now acquire a physical and materialistic dimension. Giving valued possessions to others (especially children and grandchildren) becomes a source of pleasure. The boisterous joy of a grandchild to whom one has just given one's collection of baseball cards, for instance, compensates for the sadness of loss implicit in such renunciation.

A frequent concomitant of such downsizing is a change of residence. The home in which one has lived through most of one's adulthood begins to appear too large and difficult to maintain. A move to a smaller, often single-floor residence seems desirable. At times, the shift undertaken is more radical, with the elderly moving to live near their children and grandchildren or to regions with more temperate climates.

> The well-to-do may be attracted to retirement villages, where activities are available, new friends can be found, and special provisions are made for the needs of the elderly. Poorer persons may find it convenient or financially necessary to move into special subsidized housing for the elderly. Moves to new locations often have advantages and attractions, but by and large, the maintenance of close contact with relatives and old friends is usually more important. As people age, capacities to make new friends diminish, and new friends are not likely to have the same involvement as old friends and relatives. (Lidz, 1968, p. 519)

The resulting sense of isolation is compounded by another event that just precedes a change in residence or happens at the same time. This refers to retirement from one's job. Usually, people consider and reconsider taking this step for months, if not years. Significant anticipatory mourning thus already takes place before the final day of leaving one's place of employment for good arrives. Nonetheless, a certain amount of ego-destabilization does occur at this point. There are many reasons for this. *First*, retirement precipitates the loss of a significant network for interaction with others. Upon retirement, individuals lose coworkers, bosses, and support staff in addition to customers, clients, patients, students, or other recipients of whatever services one had hitherto professionally provided. Thus, after retirement, the social sphere in which one takes part shrinks greatly. *Second*, difficult emotions are stirred up when one looks at those who would replace one in the job situation. The narcissistic envy of youth and the well-earned pride in one's vocational longevity now come in conflict as the following poem of mine, titled, *Retirement*, underscores:

> Starting his last lecture,
> he looked at the hundred or so young men and women
> sitting in front of him.
>
> A few eager to learn,
> some unable to focus,
> others spread-eagle on the cot of indifference.
>
> And suddenly he understood
> the pigeon's ambivalence
> towards e-mail. (2019, p. 5)

Third, the withdrawal enforced by retirement creates a crisis of self-esteem by eliminating an important realm from which people have so far derived so much "evidence" of their self-worth.

> Through labor, individuals gain self-esteem by witnessing their own power to effect changes or to produce goods or services.

> It is in this way that work gives individuals a sense of efficacy. When an individual loses his or her capacity or opportunity to work, he or she also loses an important experience vital to the maintenance of a "cohesive, energetic, and balanced self." (Wolf, 1997, pp. 72–73)

Such "negative" consequences of retirement do not constitute the entire picture of this period of life, however. The fact is that life after retirement can offer new and meaningful opportunities for personality growth.

> Although retirement typically means shedding occupational identities, letting go of familiar ways, and bidding farewell to one's youthful self, it can also be a highly exciting time for self-discovery, life re-invention, and discovery of the creative spirit. A life liberated from full-time employment provides unparalleled opportunity for discovering one's true passion, bringing forth hidden strengths and pursuing a free, more joyful and deeply fulfilling lifestyle. (Borchard, 2006, p. 221)

This is true for the more fortunate and active old people, a point eloquently illustrated in Gedo's (1997) playfully titled essay, "In Praise of Leisure." In others, especially those with a dependent lifestyle and a pre-existing tendency toward psychic merger with loved ones, there occurs a marked diminution of self-agency.

> Instead of voicing their own opinions, for example, they will say: "my children think such and such ...", or "as far as making a decision is concerned, see my wife". They may also merge so completely with a particular place or institution that their own self seems to have disappeared at the same time as that object: "since my retirement, I'm not worth anything anymore". (Quinodoz, 2010, p. 68)

Other old people fragment their self-images and become detached from aspects of their lives; they appear lost, absentminded, and sad. The losses they face or are about to face compound the difficulty of their existence.

Dealing with the deaths of friends, siblings, and spouses

One especially painful occurrence during old age is the death of people with whom one has had long-term associations. As one approaches the seventies and eighties, the news of such beloved individuals' deaths arrives more and more frequently. Each such loss causes "mental pain" (Akhtar, 2000; Freud, 1926d) and requires mourning. The grief is harder to bear than it might have been when there was still time to find substitute love objects. Old age precludes object "replacement";[47] the social sphere has become limited. Moreover, each loss is accompanied by the loss of a specific self-representation. As a result, one begins to feel internally poor. The deaths of siblings, old friends, and spouses cause an irretrievable depletion of the self, for in the hearts of the departed resided the shared memories of many decades. The gap created by their departure cannot be filled by more recently acquired neighbors and acquaintances.

Sibling death has accrued a reasonable amount of psychoanalytic literature but most of it pertains to the occurrence of such loss during childhood. Very few analysts have contributed to the understanding of sibling loss during adulthood and especially during old age. Engel's (1975) landmark paper on the death of his twin brother at age forty-nine is an exception. Connecting the dreams, the parapraxes, and the flashes of memory he had over the subsequent ten years, Engel offered a highly nuanced portrait of grief over sibling loss. More recently and more to the point of the discussion here, Lowy (2017) has reported upon the loss of his three-years-younger sister when he was sixty-nine years old. Here are his own words, understated, devoid of affectation, yet moving in their forthrightness:

> What did I feel, the surviving sibling? Most of the emotions and a few of the symptoms described in the literature: certainly loss and sadness; the emptiness of bereavement; empathy and sympathy

---

[47] Elsewhere (Akhtar & Kanwal, 2017), I have questioned Freud's (1917e) proposal that at the end of mourning, the lost object is "replaced" by a substitute. In my view, it is better to state that the lost object is "re-placed" (i.e., given a different sort of psychic space) than that it is "replaced." Freud (1929) himself came to see, some twelve years after writing "Mourning and Melancholia" (1917e), that no love object can and should be totally replaced.

> with her children and grandchildren whose loss, in many ways, was far greater than mine. Of course, also survivor guilt! I was now the last remaining member of our family of origin, blessed with a loving wife, children, and grandchildren, and memories of a satisfying career. Now Henny, who had been there for me, witness to the major events of my life both sad and joyful, was no longer there. Despite the strong and available social supports in my life, as the remaining survivor, I experienced brief but painful moments of feeling alone without her. These moments, inevitably, were accompanied by even briefer flashes of irrational anger—"Why did she have to get herself sick when her own family and I still needed her?" What also remains with me is the lingering regret that I could not spend more time with her, did not sufficiently encourage her to share her difficulties, and did not take a more active role in her life to alleviate her burdens and enjoy her optimism and successes. Of course, she never asked me to do any of these things. She was proudly her own person and I miss her. (pp. 95–96)

Similar wistful emotions are evoked by the loss of long-term friends. Companions and confidantes over decades, they represented the best and worst of us insofar as they had, over time, become the depository of our projections, not for maligning purposes but for us to retrieve such projections and think about ourselves in deeper ways. They bolstered our self-esteem, kept our secrets, helped us during crises, offered us the true measure of mutuality, and functioned to catalyse a "progression in the service of the ego" (Rangell, 1963, p. 28); we learned from them and grew wiser. Once they are gone, we simply cannot share the same jokes, the same memories, the same wink-inspiring "code words," and the same pleasure of watching a game, having a drink, and sharing a meal with their "replacements." The grief at their loss tends to be lifelong. A poem of mine, titled *This Is What Happened*, written soon after the death of a good woman friend, Ratula Sen (1945–2020), who also happened to be a highly accomplished singer, attests to this.

> She died last afternoon.
> But still the night came, dancing, and
> the sun opened its eyes promptly at dawn.

She died last afternoon.
But her dogs do not know this yet,
and her car is parked shamelessly on her driveway.

She died last afternoon.
But her voice is embroidered
on her aging husband's pillow.

She died last afternoon.
But that afternoon refuses to die,
threatens to live forever. (Akhtar, 2021, p. 32)

This threatened "permanence" of pain is even more striking with the fatal blow of losing a spouse during old age. Lidz (1968) noted the wide-ranging consequence of this event.

> The old person not only must assimilate the loss of a partner who has become an integral part of his or her life, but must often also adjust to becoming dependent upon others. The loss of a spouse provokes a period of stress, when an elderly person is particularly prone to incapacitation or death. The woman is usually better able to manage by herself than the man who has not learned domestic skills; but her social life is likely to become more restricted. Men are in relatively short supply; they are therefore sought as partners for widows at parties and are commonly invited out by elderly women who reluctantly learn that they must take the initiative if they wish to be accompanied. (p. 520)

While Lidz's (1968) observations might be a little dated, the fact is that men usually die earlier than women and therefore a number of elderly women end up living alone because their partners have died. It may sound sadly comical but most women approaching their seventies begin undergoing a "rehearsal for widowhood." And, they become more solicitous about their husband's (or partner's) physical health. Some of this is surely out of love but some of it is also out of self-oriented, narcissistic concerns. The admixture of "anaclitic" and "narcissistic" love (Freud, 1914c) is anyway typical in couples of long duration. Having been close, even physically merged to a certain extent, over decades results in the blurring of what is loving oneself and what is loving the other. Loving oneself becomes loving the partner and loving the partner becomes loving oneself (Chasseguet-Smirgel, 1985). Nonetheless, women suffer greater anxiety over the anticipated loss of their spouse since the likelihood of it happening is greater. Yet they seem to handle the loss better, owing perhaps to their far deeper assimilation of maternal identifications, including the "holding" (Winnicott, 1960a) function of the mother.

It is such forbearance that perhaps underlies the fact that the literature on the loss of a spouse in old age, even though meager, is almost all contributed by women analysts.[48] Notman (2014) called such transformation of a long life of mutuality and a storehouse filled with experiences, the death of a "shared history" (p. 70). Coutts (2014) said that upon the death of her husband, "I lost my sounding board, my echo, my check, my stop and finisher. I am down to one" (p. 266). And most recently, Livingston (2017) has written a most touching recollection of the first two years of her life after losing her husband in which she describes the blue parade of emotions that starts from the moment of his death, goes through the early days and the first anniversary and was still going on at the time of her writing that paper. It is a literary gem though its shine does not blind us to the fact of our own impending mortality. In fact, it might make us more acutely aware that the end is approaching.

Becoming really old, facing infirmities, and preparing to die

At age seventy-five, one becomes "officially" really old or "elderly" (US Census Bureau, 2018). Not all people become infirm at this point; those who have managed to retain good physical health still maintain a robust lifestyle. Others begin to slow down in rather obvious ways. Shakespeare (1564–1616) was well aware of such gradual decay of human existence. He wrote:

> From hour to hour
> We ripe and ripe,

---

[48] Outside of the analytic circle, the well-known writer, Joan Didion (2005), has movingly described her subjective experiences over the first year following her husband's death.

And from hour to hour,
We rot and rot,
And thereby hangs a tale.

(*As You Like It*, 1599, 2:7, 12)

And this tale has a built-in poignancy. The body refuses to perform its tasks as smoothly as before and propels one to seek rejuvenation.

> Those who recognize signs of physical deterioration—such as difficulty getting up from a chair, inability to get up from the floor after a fall, difficulty fastening buttons, etc.—engage trainers, go to fitness classes for "older" adults, and practice prescribed exercises, such as swimming or dancing. They actively try to counteract nature or at least to postpone the inevitable .... The thought of regaining past elasticity and mobility is given up only very slowly and painfully .... Thus, the men and women who avail themselves of these remedies remain disappointed. (Lax, 2008, pp. 840, 843)

One intimate area of concern is that of sexuality. The elderly often feel considerable pain and shame over their inability to have sexual intercourse; the topic becomes taboo and is avoided even by their physicians. Quinodoz (2010) has offered a word of encouragement in this regard.

> Elderly people lead us to re-situate sexual relations in the whole field of psychosexuality rather than in the domain of sexuality in the narrow sense of the word. Although this does vary from one person to another, elderly people can no longer expect their body to be at the height of its capacities, and their libido may tend to diminish. However, elderly couples who still have an active sexual life are often more and more able to perceive that sexual intercourse cannot be separated from the feelings of love it expresses. (p. 89)

Tenderness thus becomes an important feature of old age sexuality. Holding hands, a gentle kiss on the forehead, and a kind glance all begin to matter much more now. Le Goués (2006) clarifies that such tenderness is not a regression to Freud's (1912d) sexless "affectionate current."

It is informed and suffused with the memories of mature genitality that had been built by the synthesis of "affectionate" and "sensual" currents (Freud, 1912d).[49]

Further psychic devastation is caused by the frequent loss of bladder and bowel control. While this is deeply embarrassing for both men and women, the latter seem to accommodate somewhat better to it. Men deny the problem or withdraw into sulky anger.

> The situation for women is quite different. Loss of urinary control is a nuisance, but women often say simply, "Fortunately, there are ways to manage it." Women have learned from childhood on that managing is an important skill. Judging from parental reports, it seems that girls' struggles with childhood toilettraining are usually less acute and intense than boys. Their identification with mother is strengthened by their being "like" mother, and thus able to fantasize participation in her power .... They emphasize "not making a mess," being clean like mother, going to the toilet in time, managing like mother does. The fact that women, as mothers, are the ones primarily involved in the toilet training of their children focuses and reinforces their need for resourcefulness. (Lax, 2008, pp. 841–842)

Sooner or later, though, women too begin to feel the burden of getting really old. Indeed, both men and women note that they cannot hear well despite using hearing aids, get easily tired, have difficulty discerning the colors and shades of a painting they see, need a nap or two during the day, begin to fear driving, and experience low-grade anxiety on an ongoing basis. The observations by Cath (1965, 1966, 1990, 1997) eloquently capture this state of affairs.

> The senescent ego, learning from experience of life's frailties in others and recognizing its own diminished capacities, may tolerate losses which occur "on time" or be repeatedly traumatized

---

[49] In a recent contribution that draws upon literary fiction from North and South America, England, and India, Kakar (2019) has deconstructed the criss-cross between possessive desire and soulful longing in the erotic imagination of the elderly.

> (not desensitized) by the depletion, diminishment, and death of peers. By constantly scanning its unique background of depleting anchorages, the older ego prepares for its own timely decline and demise. This enhanced awareness of a vulnerable-diminished reserve in an all-too-often seemingly indifferent and changing world leads to an age-specific form of anxiety I have conceptualized as *depletion anxiety*. (1997, p. 143, italics in the original)

To his credit, Cath adds the sophisticated point that such "depletion anxiety" is new but readily becomes interwoven with the subterranean remnants of the earlier annihilation (Klein, 1932), separation (Mahler et al., 1975), and castration (Freud, 1924d) anxieties. With the dominance of disappointment, hurt, anger, and paranoia in the preexisting psychic economy, the freshly emergent depletion anxiety tends to "confirm" the infantile fantasies of punishment and retribution. The elderly cries out, "Why hast thou forsaken me?"

Such turning to religion and belief in God is frequently seen among the elderly though Cath (1965) does not include it in his reparative "triad of cathexis" at this juncture in life. According to him:

> Many, if not most, of the elders in the passage from young-old age (65–75) to old old age (over 85) find refuge in energizing one or more of three way stations. The first is the bodyself, its image and functions. The second is the past with its nostalgic reconstruction of the good old days.[50] The third is the familiar transitional world of objects ... [that become] life-long and long-life comparisons. (1997, pp. 147–148)

Cath's "triad of cathexis" captures the self-sustaining measures commonly used by the elderly. Quinodoz (2010) provides a longer and more psychologically nuanced list. This ten item list includes intensification of the pleasure one draws from: (i) the present moment, (ii) little events, (iii) utensils of daily use, (iv) people who *are* available, (v) discovering

---

[50] "Nostalgia is a bittersweet pleasure" (Kleiner, 1970, p. 11). It is bitter because it reminds one of what has been lost and it is sweet because it creates an imaginary reunion with an idealized version of that lost object or lost ambiance or lost self-representation.

the deeper traits of others' personalities, (vi) listening to silence, (vii) communicating honestly, (viii) "taking the fragility of political power into consideration and being able to distance oneself from it" (p. 103), (ix) feeling that one has little to lose, and (x) turning one's life into a work of art.[51]

However, all such stopgap measures fail to block the dawning awareness that one is soon going to die. With age, the human brain shrinks; Purkinjee cells are lost, leading to lack of coordination; Betz cells decrease, causing impairment of motor skills and, according to a 1990s Japanese study (Iyanna & Inouye, 1992), sleep spindles begin to appear from time to time during states of wakefulness, resulting in light drowsiness resembling that of infants. Such cognitive disturbance, while disturbing to all, is especially painful for highly creative individuals.

> As we become more incapacitated, we lose our ability to walk and talk, incontinence returns and we require diapers. We become edentulous and our diet consists of soft foods .... [We] become more and more dependent, increasingly helpless, and to conclude metaphorically, end up with an IV drip as an umbilical cord and we ultimately are united with Mother Earth. (Madow, 1997, pp. 165, 166)

Madow termed this epoch "the second symbiosis" as a juxtaposition to the infant–mother symbiosis described by Mahler et al. (1975). He went on to playfully turn Freud's (1920g) grim pronouncement that "The aim of all life is death" (p. 38) on its head by declaring that "The aim of all life is a second symbiosis."

This leads us into the ultimate question about adult development and, in fact, about life in general. Must the awareness of oncoming death stir up anxiety and dread in the individual or can the "assurance" that one would die provide a feeling of relief? Elsewhere (Akhtar, 2010a), I have elucidated the tension between these two views using Freud's (1923b) notion of *Todesangst* (fear of death) and the great Urdu poet Ghalib's (1797–1869) concept of *Ishat-e-qatra* (the ecstasy of a raindrop

---

[51] Shneidman's (2008) concept of "post-self" (creation of the narrative with which one wishes to be remembered after death) is pertinent in this context.

that falls on a river or ocean). Freud's declaration that "The fear of death should be regarded as analogous to the fear of castration" (1926d, p. 130) led to most subsequent analysts supporting the ubiquitous nature of thanatophobia (see Akhtar, 2010b for a comprehensive review of this body of literature). Ghalib, on the contrary, offered a view of death that emanated from ancient Hindu mysticism (Vallabhaneni, 2005), Islamic Sufism (Etezady, 2008), Zen Buddhism (Hoffer, 2015; Rubin, 2005). This perspective regarded death as a natural event without which life is incomplete and the healthy attitude toward one's approaching death as neither being manic denial nor masochistic whining but a peaceful and even welcoming acceptance. Echoes of the way Ghalib conceptualized death can be found in the works of certain philosophically inclined psychoanalysts (e.g., May, 1950; Wheelis, 1966). And, the fact is that in his personal correspondence, Freud himself refers to his approaching death in an almost endearing manner and talk about his "longing for eternal rest' (letter to Max Eitingon, December 1, 1929, cited in Eissler, 1976, p. 233).[52] Unlike Freud's *Todesangst*, this attitude of accepting mortality is more congenial to mind, largely because it is solidly grounded in reality. But I will let Wheelis (1971) iterate this truth in his characteristically somber, yet impish, voice.

> A fire becomes, not less, but more truly a fire as it burns faster. It is the being consumed that pushes back the darkness, illumines whatever there is of good in our days and nights. If it weren't brief, it wouldn't be precious. Let me say it flatly: we are lucky that we die, and anyone who pushes away the awareness of death lives but half a life. (p. 68)

Looking death squarely in the eye enhances existential sharpness and courage. This, in turn, unleashes what Joan Erikson (cited in Erikson & Erikson, 1998, p. 105) has called the "ninth stage of development" (since it follows the eight stages earlier described by her husband, Erik Erikson). Her views echo Tornstam's (2005) theory of "gero-transcendence" which

[52] Contradictions in Freud's views on death and the place of "death instinct" in the "good death–bad death" debate under consideration here have been the topic of many of my contributions (1995, 2010b, 2011b; Akhtar & Kanwal, 2017).

suggests that after eighty years of age, a noticeable shift occurs from a rational and materialistic viewpoint to a cosmic and transcendent one. Joan Erikson emphasized that the "luxury of retrospective despair" (p. 113) is given up at this point and relatedness to the world is governed by a spiritual idiom.[53] The universe appears to be a kind place and a new sort of calm appears in daily living. One quietly waits for the knock of death on life's door. Under fortunate circumstances, it is a gentle one.

Concluding remarks

In this chapter, I have summarized and updated the psychoanalytic literature on adult development. Entering some caveats at the very beginning and acknowledging variations and exceptions throughout my discourse, I have evolved a portrait of progression that takes into account biological, psychological, and sociological variables as the human life advances from its post-adolescent phase of young adulthood through midlife to old age and approaching death. I have characterized this complex sojourn as consisting of the following twelve tasks: (i) evolving a life dream and consolidating a vocational choice, (ii) establishing a wage-earner and "householder" identity, (iii) enjoying love, sex, and marriage, (iv) becoming a parent and taking on the attendant pleasures and responsibilities, (v) acknowledging and accepting bodily changes, (vi) encountering limits to material acquisitions and psychosocial achievements, (vii) adapting to a changed relationship with one's parents, (viii) letting go of children, (ix) becoming a grandparent, (x) retiring from one's job and "downsizing" one's life, (xi) dealing with the deaths of friends, siblings, and spouses, and (xii) becoming really old, facing infirmities, and preparing to die.

The important contributions of Erikson, Levinson et al., Vaillant, Benedek, Cath, Colarusso, Ross, Lax, and Quinodoz have helped me greatly in formulating the ideas presented here and to cover a rather large terrain of unfolding personality growth and maturation. As a result, I have been able to provide a fairly comprehensive and balanced understanding of adult development.

---

[53] An empirical investigation of emotions and attitudes among the elderly (Brown & Lowis, 2003) has upheld proposals made by Joan Erikson.

At the same time, I feel that three important matters remain unaddressed. These involve the need to clarify (i) that pains and pleasures accompany each stage of life, (ii) that the profusion of poetry in this essay has deep psychodynamic foundations, and (iii) that the phrase "life cycle," though commonly used in psychoanalytic literature on adult development, is erroneous. Let us now take each of these points separately for consideration.

The *first* point involves the commonly held "inverted V-shaped" model of life. This view implies that life at first goes upward in terms of success, acquisitions, accomplishments, pride, and pleasure, and such ascent is followed by a decline characterized by progressive curtailments of ability, activity, and enjoyment. Nothing can be farther from the truth. The fact is that each phase of life brings its own pains and pleasures. Young adulthood is riddled with insecurities and anxieties consequent upon competitiveness and hurry to achieve and become somebody. But it also brings the joys of sex, marital bliss, narcissistic glow of parenthood, and pride of social climbing. Midlife is rife with traumatic encounters with limits, changing relationships with parents and children, adaptation to bodily changes, and mourning over unlived aspects of the self. But it also provides the opportunity to deepen the marital relationship, enjoy the freedom from responsibilities of a young family, and take advantage of greater leisure and money usually available to oneself at this stage. Similarly, old age is troubling because of losses of family members and friends by death, diminishing physical prowess, illnesses, dependence upon others, and concern about one's own end. But it also brings the happiness of becoming a grandparent, entering a phase where one can be truly generative, and acquiring wisdom. One particular aspect of this last-mentioned attribute is the emergence of a firm "belief-in-species" (Erikson, 1975) which implies a deep and sustained conviction of the shared humanity of all people.

The *second* point has to do with the profusion of poetry in this chapter (as against the preceding chapter on child development). Such esthetic inclination was not craftily engineered; it simply evolved in the course of my writing.[54] But why? To my mind, such resort to verse reflects that

[54] The presentations at the Margaret Mahler Symposia on aging (Akhtar & Kramer, 1997) and death (Akhtar, 2010b) were similarly all replete with poetic allusions and quotes

the topics under discussion contain something deep, something moving, and even unfathomable. The merciless passage of time, illness and infirmity, and the thought of one's own death mobilize the anxieties and ecstasies consequent upon the loss of self (Lichtenstein, 1963). This, in turn, stirs up unconscious fantasies of a "second symbiosis" (Madow, 1997)—this time with the Mother Earth—and thus implicitly revives the deferred and unmentalized state of the infantile symbiotic phase. It is this affective echo that shifts the discourse from prose to poetry in the dim hope of conflating (or trading off) the approaching "second symbiosis" which is laden with ambivalence with the unquestioningly blissful "first symbiosis."

Such longing for "return" brings up the *final* point of my discourse and this pertains to the use of the expression, "life cycle," not only by Erikson (1950b), Vaillant (1977) and Levinson et al. (1978), but also by many other psychoanalysts including Mahler (1974), Dewald and Schwartz (1993), and Madow (1997). It is my contention that such designation is questionable and that the reason for this error lies in a profound anxiety about aging and death. Allow me to clarify my position. The term "life cycle" originated in the context of parasites that take many forms and need many hosts for their journey; they shed their original form and then return to it later. Take, for instance, the butterfly whose eggs hatch into a caterpillar which transforms itself into a chrysalis from which emerges a new butterfly. This is called a "life cycle." The term does not apply to human beings since their life does not end at the birth of their offspring nor do they return to an earlier stage of existence, unless, of course, one subscribes to the Hindu notion of reincarnation and repeated, even if phenotypically masqueraded, epochs of birth and death of the same individual. I believe that the use of the term "life cycle" by psychoanalysts is a manifestation of their denial of the actuality and irreversibility of death. In light of this, I suggest that we be brave and replace the phrase "life cycle" by "life span" in our lexicon. This will rectify a conceptual error and put us in deeper contact with the greatest truth about our existence, and that is that all life comes to an end from which no return is possible. We die. The curtain falls and the play is over. It is over forever.

---

from poems. These presentations are transcribed and turned into chapters of the two books cited above.

Part II

Clinical praxis

CHAPTER FOUR

Development facilitating interventions

The overview of psychic development in the preceding chapters has made it clear that (i) there is a "phase specificity" to psychological issues and any salutary or adverse external event gets translated into the emotional context of that given developmental period and, (ii) hardwired adaptive pathways as well as psychically accrued resilience lie dormant at each step of the way and can be awakened by proper environmental cues. Our customary psychoanalytic work must therefore be consistently attuned to the silently active developmental processes in the patient and to facilitating their unimpeded operation. This component of therapeutic attitude is of special importance in the treatment of patients with early deprivations and resulting ego deficits. However, for the analyst to make the needed "development facilitating interventions" and for the patient to receive and utilize them, a deep relationship must evolve within the dyad, one that is characterized by generosity and courage on the analyst's part and trust and comfort with dependence on the patient's part.

Clinical ambiance of this sort is fervently advocated by the newly emergent relational and intersubjective trends. However, a similar stance was implicit in the following statement by Winnicott (1954) made nearly seventy years ago.

> The setting of analysis reproduces the early and earliest mothering techniques. It invites regression by reason of its stability. The regression of a patient is an organized return to early dependence or double dependence. The patient and the setting merge into the original success situation of primary narcissism. Progress from primary narcissism starts anew ... [and] with the true self surrendered to the total ego, can now be studied in terms of the complex processes of emotional growth. (pp. 286–287)

To be sure, Winnicott uses Freud's (1914c) term "primary narcissism" in a somewhat different way; he uses it to describe the merging between infant and mother during the time of absolute dependence or "double dependence," as he calls it. It is regression to such intermingling of two subjectivities and growing out of it, with a strengthened true self, that constitutes the essence of analytic "cure" for Winnicott.[55]

The difference between this view and Freud's (1912e, 1914g) perspective on the therapeutic action of psychoanalysis is immediately apparent. Regression is suspect in Freud's eyes and cardinal in Winnicott's vision. Interpretation is key for Freud and affirmation central for Winnicott. No other analyst has made differences more clear than Wright (1991) who says:

> Freud, it seems to me, stands for the father with his forbidding [and?] prohibitions; Winnicott stands for the mother and her caring, nurturing, and loving. Freud is the mediator of the reality principle to which the child must adapt; Winnicott is the protector of a kinder more lenient space, which keeps reality, to some extent, at bay. (p. 280)

Clearly, our day-to-day clinical work incorporates both the Freudian "paternal element" and the Winnicottian "maternal element," but it is

---

[55] Balint's (1968) proposal that a "harmonious inter-penetrating mix-up" (p. 66) is essential for the patient to arrive at a "new beginning" also expresses the same sentiment.

the latter that belongs more squarely to the "developmental perspective" on the therapeutic action of psychoanalysis. An essentially similar point was made by Cooper (1988) in his comparison of Strachey's (1934) and Loewald's (1960) perspectives on psychoanalytic technique. Cooper noted that Strachey's model of therapeutic action is largely based on instinct theory and resistance analysis. For Strachey, the role of the analyst is that of a neutral interpreter of reality, internalized as a new object, helping to make the unconscious conscious and softening the superego. In contrast, the model analyst of Loewald offers himself to the patient as a contemporary and development-facilitating object. He works by being

> ... an emotionally related object, with an important gradient of organizational maturity between him and his patient, mindful of the patient's core of potential being, which he senses as a parent does, oriented towards the future, offering the patient opportunities to create new integrations on the armature of maturity that the analyst provides. (Cooper, 1988, p. 26)

Yet another contribution that follows the same line of thinking is that of Settlage (1994) who suggests that the analyst should fluctuate between maintaining a neutral position toward the patient's transferences and establishing a "developmental relationship" (p. 42) with the healthier sectors of the patient's personality. Through the former stance, the analyst will acquire the ability to make interpretations. Through the latter stance, he will encourage the patient's developmental initiatives.

My discourse will focus less upon those clinical interventions which aim to provide insight and make unconscious conscious (à la Freud and Strachey) and more upon those measures which consolidate self- and object-constancy, strengthen the ego, enhance the capacities for thought, enlarge the individual's scope of responsibility, and impart self-trust and hopefulness to the patient (à la Winnicott and Loewald). In categorizing such interventions, I have relied heavily on the writings of Winnicott (1954, 1956b, 1960a), Balint (1968), Loewald (1960, 1971, 1973), Abrams (1978), Herzog (1984, 2001), Settlage (1992, 1993), and Pine (1987, 1998). Adding insights drawn from my own clinical experience of four decades to this distillation of literature has yielded ten "developmental interventions." Before delving into the formal specifics of these interventions, however, I find it necessary to enter some caveats.

Some caveats

First and foremost, it must be emphasized that conducting "developmental work" does not overlook the "trio of guideposts" (Pine, 1997, p. 13) of abstinence, anonymity, and neutrality, nor does it replace other customary operations of clinical psychoanalysis. The guidelines I am going to provide about development-facilitation should not form a shrill chorus on the center stage of treatment but an important piece of its background.[56]

Second, these development-facilitating interventions might acquire greater therapeutic significance in patients with weaker psychic structures and deficient self- and object-constancy but they are also silently operative in the treatment of "neurotic" patients.

Third, some of these interventions are of special importance in the treatment of culturally and/or linguistically diverse patients. Naming of affects, provision of intellectually organizing labels for inner experiences, and validation of a changed geocultural surround are among such measures.

Fourth, utilizing development-facilitating interventions might diminish the gap between the psychoanalyst's clinical and parental postures, a shift that is unacceptable to certain practitioners. Such "resistance" can arise from theoretical convictions that decry anything other than interpretation as undue gratification of the patient,[57] hence harmful to the treatment. Or, it may originate in the analyst's countertransference and even in his or her character makeup.

---

[56] "A background," said the eminent British photographer, Lord Snowdon, "has to be just this side of being something, and just the other side of being nothing" (cited in Lacayo, 1984, p. 54).

[57] The term "gratification" has accrued negative connotations due to the ill-informed conflation of satisfying id wishes with meeting ego needs. The fact is that the "need-wish" distinction (Akhtar, 1999b) is extremely important in carrying out analytic work. Wishes are subject to interpretive resolution and appropriate displacements, needs must be met in order to sustain a meaningful therapeutic alliance.

Finally, interventions detailed below are commonplace for the practicing child analysts who feel little trepidation in using them during clinical work with their adult patients as well. Analysts who work exclusively with adults and who are theoretically or characterologically "paternal" might find that using what I have to offer is difficult. And yet, it is they who stand to benefit most by giving this material serious consideration.

Specific interventions

As stated above, I have demarcated ten specific development-facilitating interventions based upon my reading of pertinent psychoanalytic literature and upon my own clinical experience. These are (i) providing nonverbal ego-strengthening experiences, (ii) validating the patient's reality, (iii) creating the psychic space for thinking, (iv) helping the patient find words for inner experiences, (v) continuing to work peacefully despite what might seem reprehensible in the patient's material, (vi) remembering that an occasional regression is integral to development, (vii) enhancing the sense of personal agency in the patient, (viii) restraining the greed for interpretation when a thwarted developmental tendency makes its first appearance, (ix) seeing goodness in the patient, and (x) helping the patient talk about issues related to mortality and death.

Before going into the details of these interventions, an important reminder need be made. This pertains to the overall attitude of the analyst, which must accommodate the realization that psychic development is lifelong; human beings retain the potential for growth till the last breath of their lives. Freud's (1898a) conclusion that analysis is hardly feasible with older patients has undoubtedly been proven wrong as a burgeoning cadre of psychoanalysts have shown the clinical utility of such work with patients in their sixties, seventies, and eighties (Quinodoz, 2010; Segal, 1958; Settlage, 1996). That being said, we can return to looking more closely at each of these interventions.

Providing nonverbal ego-strengthening experiences

Psychoanalysts make many types of nonverbal interventions. The most common, though unrecognized, among these is their commitment to maintaining the precise time frame of the session. Beginning the session on time on a sustained basis creates a sense of confidence in the patient that when he or she arrives for a clinical appointment, the therapist will indeed be there. Like early maternal devotion supporting the infant's ego, such reliability on the therapist's part enhances "basic trust" (Erikson, 1950b) and silently erodes the patient's paranoid worldview. Conversely, ending the session on time on a consistent basis ruptures omnipotence and forces a shift of the patient's attention from the internal world to the external reality. It thus has the paternal quality of separating the child from the mother and introducing the law of limits and prohibitions.

Another nonverbal intervention consists of the analyst's exercise of "active patience" (Akhtar, 2019)[58] and the capacity to remain silent and wait even during moments of clinical turmoil. The usefulness of such posture is evident in the following clinical vignette. On the surface, it illustrates the interpretation of splitting and projective identification. However, more important to note here is that it was an unperturbed and non-intrusive silence which facilitated the unfolding of the clinical material that became the subject of interpretation.

> **Clinical vignette: 1**
>
> Rebecca Cohen,[59] a twenty-six-year-old daughter of a Holocaust survivor father, was in analysis with me. The course of early treatment was filled with anxiety-laden fantasies about her father's experience in the Nazi concentration camp. Dreaded scenarios of ethnic hatred and violence preoccupied Rebecca and this readily spread to the transference. She feared and hated me, regarded me as a Jew-hating Muslim or Arab, and suspected that I supported anti-Israeli terrorism by Palestinians. Projections of her own trans-generationally given post-traumatic Jew-Nazi split of the

---

[58] In a thorough elucidation of the concept of patience (Akhtar, 2015), I have differentiated between patience as an integral part of the analyst's attitude and the exercise of patience as a specific therapeutic intervention. The former prepares the analyst for work that would take years and is a silent accompaniment in his listening and intervening. The latter is a strategic choice to avoid intervening at a given clinical moment and wait for the right time and right reason to intervene.

[59] Names given to the patients described in this chapter are fictitious. Other measures (e.g., changing age and profession to a certain extent) have also been taken to protect the patients' confidentiality.

> self were constantly active in her relatedness with me. One day, I was hated and viciously attacked. Next day, I was deeply feared.
>
> During one session while talking of the Holocaust, she suddenly jumped up from the couch and ran to the corner of the office that was farthest from me, trembling and obviously shaken by something she had just experienced internally. Rebecca stood there crying. I remained silent. Then she found a box of tissues on the desk nearby, cleaned her face and began to look a bit composed. I did not say anything and waited patiently for things to unfold. Rebecca jumped up, sat on my desk, and asked me if I knew what had happened. I shook my head, telling her that I did not. She then revealed that she had felt that I was going to take out a knife and stab her while she was on the couch and that's why she had to get away from me. As she was narrating this, I noted that she had become much calmer. Rebecca went on to say: "You know, I have never seen your office from this end. It looks so strange … You know, what it looks like … It looks so still. Everything is unmoved, quiet. It is like a dust-cover jacket of a best-seller murder mystery. And you know what, sometimes when you can read the whole book, you find out that all the clues were already shown in the photograph on the cover of the book. Yes, your office, from this side, looks like a photograph of just that sort, with all the clues intact." Now I spoke. I said, "And, I guess, I would be the corpse in this murder scene." Rebecca smiled, stretched her arms, and aiming her clasped hands at me, made a noise indicating that she was shooting me with a gun. I responded by saying, "You know what, a little while ago you thought that I was going to kill you, and now that you have taken some distance from that position, you find yourself killing me. Look, this murder and murderer are both parts of your own self and, for the work we have mutually undertaken, it is my hope that we hold on to both these views and see how they are related to each other, where they came from, and what purposes they serve." Rebecca got off the desk, walked back to the couch, and laid down. The session continued in the "usual" way.

Yet another concept that might be included among the therapist's non-verbal interventions is that of "interpretive action" (Ogden, 1994).

This refers to the "analyst's use of activity to convey specific aspects of his understanding of the transference-countertransference that cannot be communicated to the patient in the form of verbally symbolic speech alone" (p. 135). Interpretive action differs from the analyst's use of action as a stopgap measure to establish (or reestablish) optimal conditions for analytic work. It is a nonverbal intervention aimed at putting the analysand in contact with the unconscious goings-on in his mind at the moment.

Finally, the analyst's management of his own feelings, fantasies, and impulses should also be included under the "nonverbal interventions." This is because the intrapsychic experience of the analyst, with very few exceptions, remains unverbalized during the clinical hour. At the same time, it is a powerful source of information about the patient and also about the analytic process itself. The self-care, self-education, self-scrutiny, and self-analysis as well as the occasional peer consultation or seeking supervision, however, remain "silent," as it were, though not without contributing to the progress of the treatment.

While vigilance regarding countertransference enactments is surely indicated, it should not preclude the relaxed and lambent "free-floating responsiveness" (Sandler & Sandler, 1998) needed for good psychoanalytic work. That such responsiveness may manifest in a mutually shared laughter, the playful use of a proverb, or reciting a snippet of a poem have become acceptable nowadays. But what about a benign non-erotic and fleeting physical contact between the two parties? The following clinical vignette illustrates such an occurrence and provides the opportunity to anchor it in the contemporary psychoanalytic theory.

Clinical vignette: 2

Anjali Gupta, a thirty-seven-year-old daughter of Indian immigrants to the United States, was a highly accomplished woman. She had enviable academic qualifications and was financially well-off. She was also intelligent, witty, and good-looking. All was not well with her, however. She had been raised by very harsh, religiously conservative, and xenophobic Hindu parents. In the subsequent construction of a ferocious superego, her own—mostly unmentalized—hatred of them also played a role. Anjali frequently found her life blemished, her judgment unsound, and her romantic appeal next to nothing. She was briefly married to an abusive man who drank excessively; she was dating an even more ruthlessly narcissistic man when she came to see me.

As her analysis began, I was struck by two other markers of her masochism. Despite possessing physical beauty and considerable financial resources, Anjali dressed in rather mismatched, if not shabby, clothing. And, she left each session by politely saying, "Thank you, doctor." While this incantation seemed a defense against seeing me as anything but a "doctor" (i.e., not a mother or father or brother or a potential lover), the manner in which it was uttered was striking in its submissive and self-degrading quality. It was as if I were some higher up, some majestic authority to whom she must remain subservient as a slave.

I kept this observation to myself at first and hinted at its masochistic underpinnings only when the treatment had become deeper and her self-deprecating tendency was being fleshed out in its myriad forms. With such work going on over many months, Anjali broke up with her self-absorbed and condescending boyfriend. Hesitantly, she even allowed herself to be proud of this newfound strength.

The following clinical incident happened around this time. Anjali had gone to a post office with a female coworker to mail a package related to her work. She was standing in the queue, chatting with her colleague about the intricacies of their line of work. Suddenly, a young man, some twenty-one to twenty-two years old and standing right behind them in line, interrupted their conversation. He said that the particular task they were discussing was not done in the way they thought; in fact, he opined that they were incorrect and if they wanted, he could explain to them how it was actually done. At this point in reporting this incident to me during her analytic session, Anjali said, "Guess what? I turned around and told him that he was an asshole." She seemed full of joy at this and with breathless enthusiasm raised her right hand in order to do a "high five" with me, which I reflexively did!!

Clinical moments of this sort occur in most analyses unless intellectual and/or intellectualized discourse between the analyst and patient presses for undue, if idealized, austerity. Fortunately, most analysts now realize and accept that something more than interpretation is necessary to bring about a therapeutic change. D. N. Stern et al. (1998) propose that "something" pertains to interactions that give strength to "implicit relational knowing" (p. 903) and create new and more advanced psychic organizations. Such "knowing" begins in the first year of life, is non-symbolic, and involves adaptive tasks between the infant and his caretaking environment. In the clinical situation, significant shifts in "implicit relational knowledge" (Stern et al., 1998, p. 906) occur in what have been called "moments of meeting" (Sander, 1962, 1988) or "now moments" (Stern et al., 1998). Such shifts are mostly sudden and are followed by a qualitative change in the patient's psychic organization. Stern et al. emphasize that at such moments the analyst and patient share

> mutual knowing of what is in the other's mind, as it concerns the current nature and state of their relationship. It may include states of activation, affect, feeling, desire, belief, motive or content of thought, in any combination. These states can be transient or enduring, as mutual context. A prevailing interobjective is shared. The sharing can be for the mutually validated and ratified. However, the shared knowing about the relationship may remain implicit. (1998, p. 906)

The clinical example of a "high five" between me and my patient depicts this type of clinical exchange. Its spontaneity, mutuality, and salutary consequence qualify it as a "now moment." This is amply confirmed by the following observation of Stern et al.:

> Now moments are not part of the set of characteristic present moments that make up the usual way of being together and moving along. They demand an intensified attention and some kind of choice of whether or not to remain in the established habitual framework. They force the therapist into some kind of "action," be it an interpretation or a response that is novel relative to the habitual framework. (p. 911)

The "intensified attention" that Stern et al. talk about, in my opinion, does not have to be felt consciously by the analyst; it remains mostly unconscious or preconscious. A modern, intersubjective rendition of this proposal is found in the following passage by Donnel Stern (2010):

> At these times, analyst and patient are not living as much within their individual consciousness of themselves as they are within the boundaries of a joint event that is happening between them. Of course, this is a complicated thing to say, because the joint event has everything to do with the individuals who are part of it, and requires from each participant a continuous and nuanced appreciation of his or her own experience. (p. 33)

More explicitly, a question embedded in the last part of this passage is whether to "analyze" (handle interpretively) the "now moment" after its occurrence. My sense is that unless the novel exchange gets caught up in an undetected, instinctualized, and conflictual substrate, it is better to leave such things alone. The way to know whether a "contamination" of the sort mentioned above has occurred or not is to keep an eye on the material (e.g., adverse shifts in transference, parapraxes, dreams) that follow since, as Freud (1915d) has astutely noted, "The repressed exercises a continuous pressure in the direction of the conscious" (p. 151).

Validating the patient's reality

The proposal of validating the patient's "reality" is clearly a bifurcated one. It simultaneously refers to the patient's external reality and his or her psychic reality. Freud's (1916–17) reminder that "in the world of the neuroses, it is the psychical reality which is of the decisive kind" (p. 317) is certainly true. However, it is also true that significant distortions of the "average expectable environment" (Hartmann, 1939) need the analyst's recognition as well. Without the validation of the former, the therapeutic alliance gets compromised and analysis moves in the direction of indoctrination. Without the validation of the latter, the patient's externalizations become tenacious and less amenable to interpretation. Recognition of this variable arose when psychoanalysts began treating the survivors of the Holocaust and their offspring. Auerhahn and Laub's (1987) concept of the "joint acceptance of the reality of the Holocaust" epitomized the need for explicit acknowledgment of the patient's external reality.

Such acceptance (and its over-declaration) might also be required in the cases of the long-term effects of slavery and other forms of massive group oppression. The patient's being subject to racial or religious prejudice especially needs affirmation by the analyst before the childhood determinants to the subjective experience of hurt can be analyzed.

Clinical vignette: 3

Mohammad Shakoor, a family medicine resident at a nearby hospital, sought my help soon after the infamous 9/11 terrorist attack in New York City. Mohammad was in his late twenties, single, and a recent immigrant from Pakistan. Not quite ready—psychologically and financially—to enter into a four to five times per week analysis, he agreed to come twice a week for dynamic psychotherapy. While all sorts of characterological issues (e.g., chronic rage at his violent father who beat him often during his childhood, intense ambition) were lurking in the background, the main issue that Mohammad had sought help for was his outrage that simply because he was a Muslim and hailed from Abbotabad, the city in Pakistan where Osama bin Laden was found hiding, his colleagues looked at him with unease that bordered on suspicion. He winced and bore it but fell apart when a faculty member asked him if he knew how to ride a camel and whether he had received training to be a terrorist.

Devastated by such prejudicial assault, Mohammad felt torn: he wanted to resign and go back to Pakistan but he liked his psychiatric training and looked forward to the prospect of a rewarding academic career in the future. As the first alternative was interpreted as aggression turned inwards, Mohammad decided to lodge a complaint against this faculty member to the chairman of his department. The result was pallid; no action was taken against the faculty member but Mohammad was moved to work in a more cushy and fancy clinic.

As these events were unfolding, Mohammad asked me if it were "fair" that he had to prove to others that he was not a terrorist. In no uncertain terms, I told him that this was not fair and such unfairness had hurt him deeply; I kept the link between this contemporary injustice and his father's "unfair" beating of him to myself at

> this point. Pointing that out so early had the risk of pathologizing his healthy and justified anger at the faculty members' behavior. I suggested to Mohammad that he might benefit by taking a look at the recently published book, *Good Muslim, Bad Muslim* (Mamdani, 2004), which elucidated the post-Bush splitting of Muslims into such caricatured categories. I felt he had been treated shabbily and needed an affirmation of this to stabilize his confidence in his perception and his entitlement to healthy indignation.

A similar attitude needs to be maintained toward minority candidates in psychoanalytic training which, with its Western, white, and mostly Jewish hegemony[60] can make such trainees feel out of sorts. A potential objection to "confirmations" of this sort is that it can fuel further externalization of the patient's intrapsychic conflicts. The fact, however, is that acknowledging the actual component in the patient's complaint paradoxically renders that complaint more analyzable.

Creating the psychic space for thinking

Psychoanalysis has revealed that while capacity for thinking might be hardwired, the actual act of thinking is a developmental achievement, acquired through the early interactions between a child and his parents, especially the mother. The transition from Freud's (1950a) "primary process" to "secondary process" has been operationalized by subsequent analysts with Bion (1962) being an early contributor to this realm. He proposed that "beta elements" experienced as things in themselves and cognitively undigested are transformed into "alpha elements" or thinkable thoughts by the maternal containing function and reverie. A subsequent, if indirect, derivative of this line of thinking is to be found in the work of Fonagy and colleagues (Fonagy, 1998, 1999; Target & Fonagy, 1996). These authors delineated the concept of the "reflective mode" of psychic functioning or "mentalization." This referred to the capacity,

---

[60] I have elsewhere (Akhtar, 1999a) presented the case of a Southeast Asian psychoanalytic trainee who was preoccupied with the idea that were he Jewish, he would be more successful in the field. At another place (Akhtar, 2018) I have discussed in detail the provisions that need to be made in the psychoanalytic education of minority candidates.

> to reflect upon one's own thoughts and to experience mental states as presentations. "Mentalization" evolves from the integration of the earlier mental operations called "psychic equivalence" and "pretend mode" … the former of these implies a conflation of intrapsychic and external realities and the latter a splitting-off of the two. "Mentalization," in contrast, allows for linking up the internal and external realities. Its emergence and consolidation depend heavily upon the reflection of one's mental states in the context of secure play during childhood. In other words, the growing child needs the help of parents and older siblings in order to achieve the capacity for "mentalization." The importance of "mentalization" is evident in the following ways: (1) it enables the child to see people's reactions as meaningful, since they seemed based upon feelings and thoughts; (2) it creates the possibility of distinguishing between "inner and outer truth" (Target & Fonagy, 1996, p. 462). In other words, the child becomes able to conclude that simply because someone is behaving in this or that fashion does not mean that things *are* that way; this has prophylactic value against taking over the responsibility for being maltreated; (3) it facilitates communication, since keeping others' perspective in mind improves listening, and guides responding; and (4) it enhances "intersubjectivity" … and therefore deepens life experience. (Akhtar, 2009a)

Not surprisingly then the concept of "mentalization" has been rapidly incorporated in psychoanalytic therapeutics. Therapies seeking to enhance self-reflective capacities or "mentalization based" treatment approaches are being employed with children, families, and adult patients, especially those who are thoughtlessly impulsive ("borderline"), concrete, and unable to think about their psychic lives (Allen & Fonagy, 2006; Bateman & Fonagy, 2009; Verheugt-Pleiter et al., 2008). Among the practical measures deployed in such work are commenting upon the mental content, highlighting the link between feeling and thoughts, making explicitly the steps involved in sequential thinking, naming emotions, encouraging fantasizing, verbalizing intent, and so on. Working in unison, such interventions expand (or, create for the first time) psychic space for thinking and preclude foreclosures of imagination. The following vignette provides a glimpse into this sort of clinical work.

Clinical vignette: 4

Rhonda Silverstein, a divorced chartered accountant in her late fifties, had sought help for depression, social awkwardness, and a sense of having no real purpose or person in her life. The absence of serious interest in anything—her profession, a hobby, any form of sports or exercise, literature—especially troubled her. She got herself a puppy but found it too much work and returned it to the pet shop. All in all, she found her life to be boring.

Two features stood out as her treatment began. One, that she had been brought up in a rather traditional upper-middle-class family of the 1950s where the father was busy earning money and the mother stayed home. However, her mother's being a housewife did not translate into doting upon her children. On the contrary, she neglected Rhonda and her two-years-younger brother, even though the latter had a congenital heart condition. The children were left in the care of nannies who were frequently fired. Rhonda's mother spent the day lying on a couch and watching soap operas on television; she answered her children's questions in monosyllables and never showed any enthusiasm toward their school activities. Each evening, though, she came "alive": dressed up, put makeup on, and dutifully poured two martinis as Rhonda's father pulled up his car in the driveway.

The second feature that struck me as significant involved Rhonda's manner of talking. She spoke in neatly clipped paragraphs, as it were. These contained reports of events that had taken place since our last session and almost uniformly ended with a sigh, accompanied by the word "Anyway," a pause, and then she proceeded to the next topic. Clearly, this was an indication that Rhonda felt that there was nothing further to be thought or said about the given event. This "declaration" was even more evident when she recalled something from her past. She would dutifully lay out the memory and end by saying, "Well, that is all I have to say about it," pause, and then go on to a different topic.

Curiously, though, Rhonda was aware of her superficiality and, to use her own expression, "triteness." She hated herself for being that way but couldn't help herself change; nothing retained her attention for long. As the analysis progressed, a mirror countertransference evolved: I began to feel scornful, if not contemptuous, of Rhonda's superficiality. However, I was inwardly remorseful and curious about this attitude of mine.

One day when she was castigating herself for being superficial, a question occurred to me. She is certainly shallow but do I know someone I regard as "deep"? A good friend by the name of Andy Thomson immediately came to my mind in response to this self-directed question. I now began to mentally compare Rhonda with Andy and readily became aware of the difference in their thinking patterns and their responses to my comments of one or the other variety. Rhonda responded with monosyllabic answers (like her mother!) and feigned interest in what I was saying; her nonchalance, which bordered on dismissal, was transient and she soon moved on to a topic of her own. Andy, in contrast, took whatever I said seriously, gave a thoughtful and enriching response, and implicitly invited me to think further. The difference was striking and led me to wonder about their respective childhoods. I especially felt curious about how their respective parents had handled their children's thoughts. The title of a paper that I would write in the future popped up in my mind: "A deep look at shallowness"!

I soon lost my scorn for Rhonda. More importantly, I started to make some novel interventions which had aimed at enhancing her capacity for thinking. Two examples should suffice. One pertained to my saying to her that "The next time you are about to say, 'That's all I have to say about it,' please add a few words and instead say, 'That's all I know I have to say about it.'" The other involved her use of "Anyway." I told her that hearing it brought a picture of a little girl walking in the family kitchen and coming face to face with a door that had a sign saying "Anyway" in bold red letters; the door most likely led to the dark basement. The girl got intimidated, read the sign aloud, and walked away. I suggested to Rhonda that she should bite her tongue when "Anyway" was about to come up and force herself to say at least two more sentences about the topic. I made it clear that the sort of "exercises" I was recommending would make her feel inauthentic, since these were not her words, but had the potential to deepen our work.

Similar "psychic-space-creating" interventions need to be employed when the blockage in the patient's mental functioning is related to intense drive activation. Katan's (1961) early observation that during childhood "verbalization leads to an increase of the controlling function of the ego over affects and drives" (p. 185) and Volkan's (1976) suggestion that simply naming the emotion overwhelming the patient at a particular moment is helpful in calming him down underscore this very point. At times, however, it is less a matter of identifying the emotion than of opening up the space to experience it in the first place.

Clinical vignette: 5

Lillian Strawbridge, a forty-five-year-old attorney, was in analysis with me. She was unable to decide whether to end her long but unhappy marriage to a man she found utterly uninteresting and unattractive. Their sexual life, while robust in the early days of their coupledom, had almost totally dried up. She detested his eating habits, too. What bothered her most was his inability (or unwillingness) to engage in thoughtful dialogue with her. He had turned out to be just like her father: self-absorbed, television-dependent, and careless about his health and appearance.

Lillian developed an idealizing transference to me, one that contained unmistakable though unspoken erotic elements. One day she was especially tongue-tied. With my encouragement, she quite hesitantly revealed that what she had not been able to tell me was that she wanted me to make love to her. When I asked what made it so difficult to talk about, Lillian was quick to retort back, "Because you will of course say no, and I will be humiliated." To this, I responded by saying that "If you had directly expressed your desire, I might not have said no." This made her anxious. She shot back: "You won't say yes, you can't, you are an analyst." I then told her that she was right in assuming that I wouldn't have said yes. Feeling triumphant, Lillian said, "See, I knew that you would say no." I told her that I would not have said either yes or no. She was puzzled and asked what else was there for me to say. I said, "Well, how about: 'Let us think about it,' or 'What would that do for you,' or 'Did you have a clear picture of how our erotic encounter would unfold,' and so on." To this she said, "OK, but

> in the end, you will say 'No,' wouldn't you?" My response was, "See, you are so tempted to go from 'Option A' (your desire) to 'Option C' (my rejection of that desire) that you become unwilling or unable to stay at B (imagination, fantasy, emotions, etc.)." Clearly, the purpose of such intervention was to create a space for thinking, a space for the elaboration of her desire and its origins, and a space for play, without which the therapeutic dialogue would have remained shallow, reality-bound, and meaningless.

Such slightly confrontational creation of mental space, verbalization, and elaboration of fantasy has a counterpart in the closely related intervention of providing the patient words for subjective experiences that, due to one or the other reason, remain dormant or "unformulated" (Stern, 2010).

Helping the patient find words for inner experiences

Words constitute the currency of exchange within the clinical dyad. The patient is expected to give voice to thoughts, fantasies, dreams, daydreams, bodily sensations, visual images, sudden insights, and so on, by putting them into words. The analyst listens to such material with both credulousness and skepticism. Deploying the former, he gathers "factual information" about the patient's external and internal realities. Deploying the latter, he notes undue emphasis, sharpness or roundness of cadence, unusual pronunciations, significant omissions, and so on. Attention to the patient's words thus plays a role in both credulous and skeptical listening. The former enlists the patient's help in constructing a narrative (of the patient's past, present, and immediate experience), the latter, noting how words are uttered (and used as tools, ornaments, or weapons) questions that very narrative.[61] Though a patient's silence also speaks volumes (Akhtar, 2013; Arlow, 1961; Sabbadini, 1992), his or her words are the chief allies of the "analyst's work ego" (Fleiss, 1942; Olinick, 1976).

---

[61] Greenson's (1967) reminder that "The use of clichés, technical terms, or sterile language is one of the most frequent indicators of resistance" (p. 65) is highly pertinent in this context.

This is true when the patient *has* the words to express inner contents. But when the patient lacks the ability to denote this or that affect, experience, action, or even a bodily organ, the analyst has to provide him or her with the correct words. An intervention of such sort certainly is indicated for individuals with "alexithymia" (Nemiah & Sifneos, 1970), dissociative blankness of mind, and culturally determined deficits of vocabulary.

Clinical vignette: 6

Sunita Jha, a fifty-year-old Hindu Indian woman has been raised by an instinctually repressed (and repressive) family in South Africa and speaks mainly in English during her analysis. As early fears of criticism and rejection are interpretively softened, a devalued self-image emerges. While childhood experiences of prejudice due to skin color are emphasized at first, analysis gradually reveals profound rejection by her mother, a rejection centering upon her being female. Work along these lines relaxes her further and she occasionally begins to speak in Hindi, her mother tongue. During one such session, she reveals that she does not know the word for the female genital in Hindi and feels that it would help her to acquire this knowledge. Issues of maternal transference (i.e., can I label her body parts for her?; do I know and accept that she has female genitalia?, etc.) are clearly evident and I handle them in the customary analytic fashion.

However, in a later session, she earnestly asks me to tell her the word. Suddenly, I find myself experiencing a dual dilemma. One was a purely technical dilemma, that is, what would be the process-related pros and cons of telling her the word as against inquiring as to why she wanted to know it from me, and so on. The other dilemma which caught me by surprise involves my personal morality, as it were. Can I even utter the word in my mother tongue (spoken Hindi and Urdu have the same word for the female genital) in the presence of a woman? Experiencing the inhibition outlined nearly a century ago by Ferenczi in his paper on obscene words, for a moment, I become tongue-tied. Then working through the inner block and in the spirit of "developmental work" that includes occasionally providing patients with words for what is hard for them to express, I decide to tell her that the female genital is called *choot* in Hindi. I am aware of the potential transference gratifications in this intervention but the subsequent flow of our work confirms my hunch that letting her hear the word from me would facilitate and not impede our access to that material.

Another manner in which "wordplay" enters the clinical dyad is the mutually agreed-upon creation of words and phrases. Often such neologisms help bridge the gap between the patient's and the analyst's approximate but different understanding of the former's subjective experience.

Clinical vignette: 7

Julie Richards, a thirty-two-year-old woman with a deeply ensconced borderline personality organization (identity diffusion, splitting, object hunger, search for a perfect person to merge with, and intense rage) would explode or retreat into stony silence each time I would announce my vacation or even a day or two away from clinical work. A "confusion of tongues" occurred between us at such times. I pointed out her rage (at my freedom and separateness). Julie emphasized her mental pain (at what felt to her as abandonment and indifference to her welfare). After many instances of disagreement, we ended up with a conclusion that felt mutually satisfactory. We agreed to term her reaction neither as "pained" nor as "angry" but as "paingry." The neologism helped synthesize the "owned" and "disowned" facets of her subjectivity and enriched the therapeutic alliance she had with me.

In contrast to sharing (Clinical vignette: 6) and coining (Clinical vignette: 7) of words to help mentalize unformulated experience and/or strengthen therapeutic alliance are instances where it is not a word but its pronunciation by the patient that pulls the analyst's attention. In homo-lingual patients, odd and highly unusual pronunciations of commonly used words might require tactful questioning; this can, at times, lead to significant information about early identifications and dis-identifications. However, in bilingual patients, especially those who are fresh immigrants and do not adequately know the language of their new land, the analyst might need to inform the patient of the correct pronunciation.

Clinical vignette: 8

Edward Kim, a twenty-nine-year-old South Korean immigrant psychiatry resident, entered psychotherapy with me for his intense vulnerability to shame and the consequent avoidance of heteroethnic company and learning new skills. Having been in the United States for only two years by the time he came to see me, Ed was not comfortable with going to lunch with his "American" peers; he specially dreaded the loud and crowded Jewish deli which his buddies loved to go to for a take-out meal. He felt out of place and out of sorts since he was not familiar with the menu and did not understand what some of the items on it were.

Just around this time, he reported to his Jewish analyst his dilemma whether he should or should not wish the latter "Happy Chanukah" as the holiday was approaching soon in time. While his hesitation (and the ambivalence underlying it) needed analytic exploration, a more urgent matter pertained to his pronunciation of the word "Chanukkah"; Ed pronounced it with a hard "ch" (like that of "character" or "chronology"). Realizing the possibility that he might utter it that way in front of his Jewish classmates and be exposed to shame, Ed's analyst decided to tell him that "ch" in the festival's name was not pronounced that way and the holiday was referred to as "Hanukkah," with emphasis upon the first syllable. The analyst was aware of his parental protectiveness in doing this and felt a little uneasy that his own colleagues would find such an intervention "non-analytic," but overcame that resistance in the service of his patient and with the knowledge that any "adverse" effects of this "gratification" could later be analyzed.

An objection to this type of intervention is that it directly gratifies the patient's hunger for a good parent and represents the analyst's counter-transferential "dis-identification with the aggressor" (Gabbard, 1997), with the consequent failure to analyze the patient's hunger, anger, and fantasy to undo the past. A counter-argument to such thinking is constituted by the acknowledgment that in the treatment of children, borderline patients, and individuals with others types of ego impairments, the patient's "benevolent parental identifications" (Stone, 1967) deposited in the analyst are activated, the "analyst's pedagogic function" (McLaughlin, 1996) becomes active, and a "continuum of parental functions" (Hausner, 2000) gets infused in the analytic work. Needless to add that such "protective" measures must not be allowed to become a predominant mode of the analyst's functioning. Ego support is not a replacement for the analysis of transference; it is a stopgap measure so that the patient can gain (or regain) a strong footing for deeper exploration of his mind. The provision of ego support, anticipatory protectiveness, and occasional educative measures "provides auxiliary regulation pending improvement in the patient's self-regulatory capability" (Settlage, 1994, p. 48).

Continuing to work peacefully despite what might seem reprehensible in the patient's material

No better preamble to this subsection exists than the following passage from Pine's (1998) remarkable monograph titled *Diversity and Direction in Psychoanalytic Technique.*

> The analyst's continuing to attend to and work with the patient matter-of-factly and appreciatively (Schafer, 1983), even in the face of what the patient may experience as reprehensible or shameful confessions, automatically imparts to the patient a measure of respect and esteem through the analyst's maintenance of a basic working attitude without the need for any special reassurance. (p. 210)

This important clinical observation is illustrated by the following three clinical vignettes, the first of these being by far the most "powerful," hence posing a greater challenge to the analyst's equanimity.

Clinical Vignette: 9

After spending months talking about the atrocities he was subjected to during the Vietnam War, Philip Hockenberry, a

> thirty-five-year-old Army veteran, approached the deep sense of remorse at his own cruel acts in that nightmarish setting. This turned out to be the most difficult phase of our work. His was a profound sense of shame and remorse, his "confessions" halting, soaked with tears, and, at times, accompanied by hitting himself in my presence. My approach in such moments was to stay still, listen patiently, make gentle empathic remarks, and at times point out how the state-sanctioned relaxations of conscience permit transgressions that, upon return to "civilized morality," can appear horrifyingly unethical to oneself.
>
> During one such session, Phil recounted the following event: One quiet afternoon when no gunfire was going on and no overt hostilities were in sight, he spotted a pregnant woman in the distance. Looking at her intently, Phil wondered if he shot her protruding belly, whether the fetus would fly upward or fall on the ground. The curiosity grew by the minute and finally he decided to see what would actually happen and shot her in the belly. The woman screamed, fell on the ground, and soon died; the fetus could not be seen as the woman had fallen face-forward. Phil's "experiment" had failed.
>
> Recalling this years later in his treatment, Phil was overwhelmed with remorse, which was readily transformed into self-directed rage. He wept, loudly cursed himself, and punched the nearest wall with great force. I was dumbfounded. It took me a long time to overcome my own rattled state and began feeling anger at this barbaric act. This gradually shifted to empathy with his remorse and, on the broader level, a tragic awareness of what war can do to human mental functioning. I continued to see Phil for many months afterward.

While this incident was truly dramatic and grotesque, the analyst's capacity for "survival" (Winnicott, 1963a) is tested by less "repulsive" revelations as well.[62]

---

[62] I have elsewhere (Akhtar, 2009a) elucidated the myriad origins of such capacity in the analyst.

Clinical vignette: 10

Jules Levin, a fledgling businessman in his late forties, had had a painful childhood. Born with a visible deformity of his face, he was also short of stature. Throughout his childhood, he was mocked by his father and, over time, became acutely vulnerable to shame. He started keeping his thoughts and actions secret. One secret that came out early in his treatment was his sexually touching his younger sister while she was fast asleep; this began when Jules was eleven years old and lasted for a few months. In reporting his late-night excursions to me, Jules felt shame but was unable to recall (or speculate about) his fantasies and expectations in doing this. He simply felt he had to do something odd, something bizarre, to have an alive psychic self since his normal self had been decimated by his cruel father (and ignored by his mother).

During one session, while talking freely about how he sought vitality in lieu of his depressive existence, he suddenly stopped. Something had clearly come to his mind that was difficult to talk about. With gentle interpretation of his fears of my reaction, Jules became able to talk again. He revealed that he has the shameful habit of picking his nose and then eating his snot. I could sense a profound sense of sadness and solitude connected to Jules' behavior. I responded by saying that there seemed to be some connection between his touching his sister's genitals and his eating his snot; a certain audacity characterized both these behaviors. My voice was peaceful and conveyed my deep interest in his emotional life. Jules relaxed and began talking more fluently.

The following vignette also illustrates the clinical benefits of patience and non-judgmental attitude of the patient's exposure of his shame-laden aspects.

Clinical vignette: 11

Norman Liebowitz, a thirty-two-year-old internist from a regional medical center, came to see me for "depression." From all external appearances, he seemed successful: he was young, handsome, financially stable, and physically healthy. He was also happily married and recently had become a father. It was this last epoch that I felt had, paradoxically, triggered the depression he was feeling. Support to this line of thinking was given by the account of prior masochistic mishaps associated with his graduation from college and from medical school.

As the interview proceeded, Dr. Liebowitz abruptly stopped and said while all he had said so far was true, there was something else that was troubling him even more. This "something" had been with him for many years but he had never been able to talk about it with anyone. I responded by gently encouraging him to say more about what this hidden problem was and also about the concerns that had led him to keep it a secret. After some hesitation, Dr. Liebowitz revealed that he liked to chew upon cats' nails. He would frequent the houses of friends and acquaintances and, at times, scout the neighborhood to find a cat. Holding the animal up in his arms, he would bite off a chip from its nails. He kept these bits and pieces in a glass vial and chewed upon them at his leisure. As the interview progressed, a second interaction with cats emerged. He liked to bring a cat's face very, very close to his own face and then breathe in the air that came out of the cat's nostrils. Both these acts gave him deep gratification though he also worried about their apparent oddity and did not quite know what to make of them. The next day, while describing his family background, Dr. Liebowitz came upon the topic of his mother. He sighed, saying: "You don't want to know about her. She is so controlling and so intrusive that I cannot describe. She lives about a thousand miles from here but I constantly feel her claws digging in to me." As he said this, he grabbed the upper part of his left arm with his right hand, making the latter appear like a claw, and dug his nails into the skin. Seeing the connection between the biting off of a cat's nails and the alleged claw of his mother on his arm, I said: "Did you notice what you just said?" He was puzzled. "What?" he responded. I said, "What do you make of your using the word 'claws' in connection with your mother and how do you connect her 'claws' with a cat's nails?" He was dumbfounded but gradually became somber and began to talk about his chronic difficulty of maintaining an optimal distance from his mother. With further elaboration during the session, the biting off of the cat's

> nails and breathing the air coming out of the cat's nostrils could be seen to symbolize the two sides of this distance–closeness conflict. As this clarification settled in our dialogue, I could see him become more animated and curious about his intrapsychic life.

What all three clinical vignettes cited above have in common is this: as the patient who has taken the risk of revealing aspects of himself that he regards as shameful, the analyst's retention of a matter-of-fact stance (without overt and unnecessary reassurance) makes the patient feel safe, more able to divulge intrapsychic material and better participate in the interpretive step that follows the initial "affirmative" (Killingmo, 1989) posture of the analyst.

Remembering that an occasional regression is integral to development

Development is not linear. Psychoanalytic paradigms of various types (e.g., Freudian oral, anal, phallic, and oedipal; Kleinian paranoid and depressive; Winnicottian illusion and disillusion; Mahlerian symbiosis and separation–individuation) give an impression that psychic development proceeds in a reliably progressive manner. In actual life, this is hardly the case. Oscillations between progressive and regressive trends are typical and can be discerned not only during the childhood phases of development but adulthood as well. Freud (1913i) described obsessional neurosis as reflecting a regression from the oedipal to the anal phase dynamics; far more important was his 1914 addition of a passage of *The Interpretation of Dreams* (1900a) which distinguishes between three types of regression: topographic, temporal, and formal. The second of his concepts, namely "temporal regression" is of great consequence to our understanding of psychic development. It proposes that developmentally earlier forms of mentation and behavior can reappear in the course of life; this may be triggered by fluctuations in drive pressures or events in external reality. Within the context of "temporal regression," Freud distinguished between regression in regard to the object, the aim, and the ego attributes.

Subsequent analysts elaborated on these ideas. However, Blos' (1968) proposal of "regression in the service of development" is especially pertinent to the matter under consideration here. Blos noted that revisiting an early psychic position with the help of a more informed and resourceful ego facilitates the working through of them. This tendency is most marked in adolescence but may also be evident at other times, for instance during midlife. Regardless of timing, keeping the fact that regression is integral to development helps the analyst bear the unexpected appearance of psychic postures that seem to have been mastered and renounced by the patient.

Clinical vignette: 12

Bob Henderson was an illustration par excellence of what William Niederland (1968) has termed "survivor guilt." At the age of four, he lost his much-hated, two-years-younger sister. At age ten, he lost his mother to cancer. And, at age thirteen, a freak accident when he and his best friend were playing led to the latter's death. Not surprisingly, Bob's subsequent development and all his adult life, before he sought help, was characterized by unrealized ambitions, failed dreams, and being "wrecked by success" (Freud, 1916d); a tragedy followed each time he achieved a goal. Bob's romantic relationships were similarly disastrous. He had been repeatedly involved with socially marginal and mentally unstable women. One long-term girlfriend was not at all interested in sex while another mercilessly mocked him for his passion for collecting baseball cards. And so on.

With analytic insights and working through his early trauma (as well as his fantasies of having caused the deaths of his sister, mother, and friend), Bob began to feel better about himself. He started to take better care of himself, obtained a job promotion, and became able to accept compliments from friends and coworkers without wincing. For the first time, he got involved with an "appropriate" and kind woman though this relationship did not last very long because she decided to leave town to be close to her parents; her father had had a stroke and her mother needed help managing him.

As Bob's analysis went on, I felt some relaxation on my part, assuming that we had mostly worked through his masochistic need for self-punishment. Just then, Bob "found" another

> narcissistic and cruel woman with three children of her own and fell madly in love with her. Privately, I wondered if this regression was somehow mobilized by the resurgence of his chronic guilt or was it a result of his unconsciously picking up *my* pleasure in his improvement. Nonetheless, I had to bear this aggression and continue the usual analytic work with fortitude and patience.

Clearly, the analyst has to consider that such regression might be due to a "negative therapeutic reaction" (Freud, 1923b), in a guilty return on the patient's part to suffering.[63] On the other hand, a regression of such sort can also be viewed as reflecting the fragility of newly acquired ego positions. This, in turn, can be regarded as inherent to psychic development and as a phenomenon that will need to be respectfully tolerated and repeatedly worked through. Pertinent here is Freud's reminder that under such circumstances, "The doctor has nothing else to do than to wait and let things take their course, a course that cannot be avoided nor always hastened" (1916d, p. 155). Yet another matter to be kept in mind is that while analysis encourages regression, it also activates progressive trends. In fact, the analytic setting might provide certain patients the first access to the latter. In Abram's (1978) words:

> Such access would be valuable on several accounts. For one thing, it is worthwhile to have a conscious awareness of any area of unconscious activity; for another, aiding the ego in the distinction between the progressive and regressive may result in a further sharpening of the expressions of the transference neurosis; and lastly, by rendering a progressive potential into consciousness, one might facilitate the emergence of experiential building-blocks necessary for development. (p. 397)

All in all, the analyst must keep an eye on both progressive and regressive trends and be prepared to uphold the former and bear the latter.

---

[63] Besides unconscious guilt, "negative therapeutic reaction" can result from identification with a masochistic parent, separation-related anxieties, and envy of the therapist's helping capacities.

Needless to add then, the analyst must sooner or later take an interpretive approach vis-à-vis the forces that mobilized the aggressive trend.

Enhancing the sense of personal agency in the patient

The emergence of a sense of "intentionality" around three months of age (Hartmann, 1939) lays the groundwork for the subsequent development of "a representation of the self as intender (agent) coordinated with a representation of an action" (Lichtenberg, 1983, p. 63). This step during toddlerhood prepares the child for the gradual "ownership" not only of his or her actions but of the fantasies and motivations underlying them. The child now becomes capable of experiencing intrapsychic conflict, a capacity that is sharpened by the later passage through the oedipal and adolescent phases.

Such consolidation of intentionality and self-agency is crucial to participation in psychotherapy. In its absence, one merely complains of external interferences and random mishaps. To be sure, gray areas do exist between having and not having a clear-cut sense of agency. Individuals raised in collective cultures that place emphasis upon a "familial self" (Roland, 1988) continue in their adulthood to display "seemingly inoptimal individuation" (Akhtar, 1999a, p. 130) and do not fully "own" their intrapsychic conflicts. They lack the firmness of self-boundaries typical of Western individuals and are prone to experience aspects of their conflicts as arising from their relational matrix and not from within themselves.[64]

Geocultural difference, however, is not the only determinant of a weakness of self-agency. Dorpat's (1976) distinction of "object relations conflicts" and "structural conflicts" is relevant in this context. The individual with the former type of conflict experiences opposition between his own wishes and his internalized representation of another person's wishes. For instance, he says: "I want to do this but my departed mother's soul would be hurt." This is in contrast to the person with a "structural conflict" who says: "I want to do this but I should not." Or, "I want to do this but I also do not want to do this." The former individual "owns" only one side of

[64] I have elsewhere (Akhtar, 1999b) delineated the guidelines for dealing with this problem.

his conflict and experiences the other side as emanating from someone else. The latter individual "owns" both vectors of his conflict. To extend Anna Freud's (1965) phraseology which equated "structural conflicts" with "internalized conflicts," object relations conflicts can be termed "partially internalized conflicts." Such conflicts usually represent tensions and trauma arising from a less differentiated of the psychic structure.

However, culturally determined variables and psychostructural levels of organization do not exhaust the list of variables that lead an individual to disown his or her intrapsychic goings on. Defensive operations of repudiation, negation (Freud, 1925h), and passivity may also result in such an outcome. While this poses a challenge to the therapist's work ego, it may be better to provide a few pertinent clinical vignettes before delving into the interventions directed at undoing such psychic disownment and enhancing the patient's sense of personal agency.

Clinical vignette: 13

Eliza Frank was in her early sixties when she began treatment with me. She had had an earlier analysis that lasted a little over ten years and was mostly a failure. It left her feeling as self-critical and as envious of her older brother as she had been. Eliza came to me a few years after terminating this treatment. She presented with constant self-criticism and unrelenting comparison of herself with her brother; in reality, she was more successful than he was but somehow continued to feel that his demonstrations of superiority were valid.

As our work progressed and the childhood roots as well as the defensive functions of her self-castigation were unmasked, hostile feelings toward her parents who over-indulged their male offspring began to surface. Self-criticism diminished. A careful look, however, revealed it had only taken a new shape: "pangs of regret," as Eliza called them.

Such "pangs" consisted of her suddenly remembering something from years past and wishing that she could have done things differently then. An important feature of these pangs was their feeling totally out of her control; they appeared out of nowhere, it seemed. The necessary first step in her coming to grips with them consisted of helping her "own" their origin. In other words, I needed to help her recognize that it was she who was the "author" of these

> pangs. Only by establishing this, could we decipher the paradoxical admixture of masochism and omnipotence underlying such regret.

This clinical vignette opens up significant vistas for discussing the not infrequent denial of self agency, the defense of passivity, and the associated sense of being victimized by parts of one's own mind. However, before addressing these matters, I offer another clinical vignette to highlight the phenomena under consideration.

> **Clinical vignette: 14**
> Upon being told by her psychotherapist, Dr. Nathaniel Graham, that he was soon finishing his psychiatry residency and would be leaving town, Anna Kleber, a twenty-five-year-old college student, became teary and pensive. When the therapist commented upon the sudden change of affect and invited her to talk about it, Anna said the following: "The word 'abandonment' comes to mind but it is not right since you are not deliberately abandoning me. You are finishing your training and have to get another job, I know." Clearly, she was deploying two defensive maneuvers here: (i) turning the active sense of being dropped to the passive entry of the word "abandonment" in her mind, and (ii) seeking refuge in the reality aspects of the situation to keep her feelings in abeyance.
>
> As a supervisor of this case, I said that it would have been worthwhile to underscore the use of her defenses, especially her "decision" to experience abandonment as a mere word (isolation) and as somehow having "come to mind" (turning activity into passivity) and how doing so might have made her see that her therapist was not afraid of strong feelings in the room. This, in turn, would have facilitated her "owning" and expressing those feelings and their deeper origins.

Both my patient (Clinical vignette: 13) and my supervisee's patient (Clinical vignette: 14) demonstrated the defense of passivity vis-à-vis certain aspects of their mental life. They did not feel responsible for their own thoughts. Eliza got "pangs of regret" and Anna felt that the word "abandonment" simply popped up in her mind. How is such psychic repudiation best handled?

First, it must be acknowledged that "We often initiate treatment by telling the patient 'say whatever comes to your mind'. So perhaps this invites his or her phrase: 'it just came to mind'" (Sybil Houlding, personal communication, May 25, 2021). In other words, the patient's passive presentation might be co-constructed and reflect the patient's "freedom of free association" (Kris, 1996, p. 9).

Second, an intervention that might push the therapeutic dialogue forward might involve the analyst's saying, "Alright, now that this has come to your mind, what do you think about it?" If the patient then denies any responsibility for his or her thought, the analyst might underscore that and ask about the need for such repudiation.

Third, Schafer's (1976) concept of "action language" is also of use in such circumstances. When a patient claims that he got this or that idea out of nowhere, the analyst must avoid the use of nouns in response and instead use verb-adverb formulations. This would eradicate the distinction between motivational forces and resulting thoughts. All that passes within a clinical dyad would then be action: preparatory, preliminary, constitutive, and actual.

Finally, it should be remembered that all "interpretation of the present conflict is tactical rather than strategic—it is preparatory" (Etchegoyen, 1999, p. 428). Thus unmasking "pangs of regret" or the fact that the word abandonment "comes to mind" are to be regarded as passive ways of saying "I tortured myself with regret" or "I think of abandonment when you tell me that you're leaving." These latter statements are then to be pursued "backwards" toward their origins in their experiences and fantasies of the past.

Working in unison, these four measures, combined with the demonstration that the analyst never speaks in a passive voice, can help the patient evolve a greater sense of personal agency and "ownership" of his or her internal life.

Restraining the greed for interpretation when a thwarted developmental tendency makes its first appearance

Subscribing to the long-held dictum that interpretation is a sine qua non of clinical psychoanalysis, most analysts respond to the patient's material at first by empathic listening and then by attempts at clarification and interpretation. This is especially true when patients' associations take an unusual turn, an enactment occurs, and demand is made upon the analyst to act in this or that manner and in essence change his or her therapeutic attitude. While generally acceptable, the desire to interpret can, at times, turn into a "compulsion to interpret" (Epstein, 1979). The unconscious greed that propels such compulsion is especially aroused by demanding, withholding, and persistently rejecting patients. Issacharoff (1979) observes that under such circumstances, if the analyst suppresses his greed, it becomes difficult to retain an empathic link with the patient. However, if the analyst gives in to his greed, he is experienced by the patient as hurried and intrusive.

This clinical dilemma is forcefully mobilized when the patient makes an unexpected and unusual demand. The notions of "acting out" (Freud, 1905e, 1914c), "acting in" (Zeligs, 1957), and "enactment" (Ivey, 2008; Levinson, 2003) readily pop up in the analyst's mind and push him toward making an interpretation right away or after some attempt at clarification. However, a developmentally informed alternative exists here. This pertains to regarding the emergence of an unusual demand as the manifestation of a renewed or experienced-for-the-first-time sense of entitlement; Kramer's (1987) proposal that such a situational tendency to act as an "exception" is often due to the patient never having experienced a normal childhood phase of specialness and entitlement over his or her parents. In Kramer's view, this sort of attitude on the part of the patient was transient and reflected a positive consequence of the interpretive work that preceded it.[65] Keeping this possibility in mind makes it possible for the analyst to retrain his "greed for interpretation," let the material evolve at its own pace, and even provide a modicum of gratification to the patient.

Clinical vignette: 15

Rose Perry, an extremely ascetic, depressed, and socially isolated woman with a childhood history of profound neglect and abuse

[65] As can be clearly noticed, Kramer's (1987) explanation is in sharp contrast to the original proposal of Freud (1916d) that children who suffered "an unjust disadvantage" (p. 313) such as a congenital defect or death of parents grow up to be adults who feel deserving of being spared from the ordinary rules and regulations of life.

> made a request of me in the third year of her psychotherapy. I had moved into a new office and the changed seating arrangement forced her to face a certain painting that she disliked. She requested that I put it elsewhere in the office. While curious about the potential meaning of the request, I sensed something different at work here. The patient had begun experiencing entitlement! I therefore responded by saying, "It is encouraging that you can allow yourself to demand something of me. Now, as it happens, I rather like the painting and its location so I would not move it altogether. However, in keeping with your desire, I will take it off the wall before each of your sessions so that you will not have to look at it." I reliably did so for about three or four months, after which she said that it was fine with her if I stopped the practice. (Deeper understanding of the request came much later.)

Noticeable in this bit of clinical interaction is the absence of interpretation. But I hasten to add that I had not lost or abdicated my role as a skeptical listener (e.g., what makes the painting undesirable to look at?, what does she "really" expect me to do?, what would it mean to her if I removed the painting and what would it signify if I did not?, and so on); I had only put it aside for a while and decided to act from an "anagogic" (Silberer, 1914) and "affirmative" (Killingmo, 1989) point of view. My approach was thus "constructivist" (Piaget, 1963) and not ontogenetic. In other words, it took into account that "unconscious *progressive* trends are also activated in the analytic process" (Abrams, 1978, p. 347, italics in the original). My approach paid attention to the possibility of emerging new levels of ego integration and did not focus upon tracing the old origins of my patient's behavior (e.g., childhood deprivation of healthy entitlement). Such "developmental interventions" (Abrams, 1978) provide the patient a greater access to the silent progressive trends activated by the treatment. They underscore the dialectical relationship between the interpretive resolution of psychopathology and the resumption of psychic growth. With each undoing of some aspect of pathology, there is the opportunity for resumed development in that area, and with each such developmental advance, there is an enhancement of the patient's tolerance for the exposure of unacceptable, anxiety-provoking wishes and fantasies (Settlage, 1994).

Seeing goodness in the patient

Like the sculptor who can envision the statue hidden in a rock, the analyst sees the potential strengths of his patient. This has a developmentally salutary impact upon the patient who strives for correspondence and proximity with the analyst's "vision" of him. In Loewald's (1960) words,

> The parent–child relationship can serve as a model here. The parent ideally is in an empathic relationship of understanding the child's particular stage in development, yet ahead in his vision of the child's future and mediating this vision to the child in his dealing with him. This vision, informed by the parent's own experience and knowledge of growth and future, is, ideally, a more articulate and more integrated version of the core of being that the child presents to the parents. This "more" that the parent sees and knows, he mediates to the child so that the child in identification with it can grow. The child, by internalizing aspects of the parent, also internalizes the parent's image of the child—an image that is mediated to the child in the thousand different ways of being handled, bodily and emotionally. (p. 229)

The caveat that needs to be entered here pertains to the fact that the analyst's vision must be primarily guided by his empathic knowledge of the patient and not by his falsely generative hunger for clinical offspring. Assessment of "analyzability" and—on the other temporal pole of the clinical scenario—of readiness for termination provide two clear instances where the analyst's impartial and yet developmentally informed vision plays a significant role in technique. Vis-à-vis patients' inherent "goodness" per se, however, the concept of "anagogic interpretation" (Silberer, 1914) is far more apt. This refers to a mode of decoding symbolism that brings out its universal, transcendent, and ethical dimension. Unlike the usual psychoanalytic tendency to decipher symbols along personal and sexual lines, *anagogic* (Greek for "to bear upwards") interpretations elevate the concrete into the spiritual. For instance, from a traditional analytic stance, a dream of buying a big house might be seen as related to a competitive wish, a desire to expand one's family, or a soothing defense against feelings of inferiority in other realms of life, and so on. From an anagogic perspective, however, the same dream can be seen as expressing a desire to expand one's mind so that one can include concerns and problems faced by others; the dream will be viewed as a statement of blossoming civic-mindedness.

Less high-minded and yet pertinent to the analyst's seeing "goodness" in the patient are Winnicott's (1956b) and Casement's (1991) views on antisocial tendency and unconscious hope, respectively. These perspectives impel the analyst to discern a streak of optimism and search for redress in provocative behavior. As a result, what seems phenomenologically "bad" turns out to be developmentally "good."

Clinical Vignette: 16

Jack Lieberman, a deeply traumatized but highly successful businessman in his mid-sixties, suffered from chronic self-loathing and from uncertainty despite frequent accolades from esteemed others and almost daily hobnobbing with renowned members of society. He had grown up with constant ridicule and abuse by his somewhat sociopathic older brother who, in Jack's perception, was secretly admired by his parents. Moreover, Jack never felt truly appreciated by his parents, no matter what he achieved or accomplished. As an adult, he often derided himself as being inferior to others, unable to love, have empathy for this or that person, and forgive others for their blemishes. He dismissed his own cognitive and linguistic talents, especially in the realm of administration and business negotiations, with an air of nonchalance, if not derision. He experienced disbelief when his wife praised his appearance and called him a "good man."

In one of his sessions, Jack reported the following incident. He was taking a stroll on the boardwalk and caught a glimpse of some teenage boys and girls playing volleyball on the beach. The girls were nubile and skimpily dressed. Jack thought that he would want to "fuck them right there" while the boys who were playing with them seemed to be devoid of such lust; they seemed to be innocently playing volleyball. Jack was filled with a wistful longing for the simplicity of the heart he felt he had lost along the way and also with contempt for himself. As he narrated this experience,

> I found myself empathizing with both: what appeared to be his sexual (and oral) greed as well as his superego attack against his libidinal impulses. However, to my mind, a more important aspect of the entire experience was his capacity to "read" the boys' innocence. As I thought more, it became clear that this was based upon an admixture of (a) intact reality testing and plausible perceptions; (b) empathic resonance with the experience of those boys, and (c) a projection of his own repudiated "goodness" into them. I therefore said, "I can sense your wistfulness and, to a certain extent, understand your criticism about your hunger. What puzzles me, however, is that you say nothing about how you were able to recognize those boys' 'goodness' from afar. What do you think made that possible?"

In making this intervention, I was trying to help Jack become cognizant that the innocence he had attributed to the boys on the beach was, at least in part, his own repudiated goodness. My conjecture was based on the fact that Jack had not allowed any possibility that even one of these boys (or all of them, to a certain extent) might be experiencing lust and sexual greed. He had turned them into "all good" creatures and himself into a despicable representative of humanity. What he could not see and/or hold on to within himself (his own goodness) was what my intervention intended to bring back to him. It was, in effect, an extra-transference interpretation of his "positive projective identification" (Hamilton, 1986) and, in its unmasking and knowledge-enhancing aspect, reflected what Wright (1991) has called "the paternal pole of psychoanalytic technique."

Helping the patient talk about issues related to mortality and death

Most psychoanalysts think that only orphaned adults, terminally ill patients, those recently bereaved by the loss of a loved one, and elderly analysands talk of their own death during their analyses. This is not true. References to one's mortality appear in all analyses. For instance, when a patient in termination phase talks about death, the allusion is not only metaphorical. The patient is saying to the analyst: "Look, I am leaving treatment for good and we have not talked about an extremely important topic yet. Can we please do it now?" Or, when such a patient laments that he shall never see "this office" again, the analyst might consider it as a displaced fragment of the patient's mourning over separation from him *or* the analyst might take it as a cue that the patient is prepared to talk about the day when he will not be able to see "this whole world" ever again. Listening to the terminating patient's talk of death in a skeptical fashion yields interventions about separation and mourning. Listening to the same material in a credulous fashion permits an exploration of the patient's feelings and fantasies about death.

Once the patient's concern with mortality has been discerned, the next step is to help him get in deeper contact with feelings and fantasies surrounding it. Lest such a recommendation appear "un-analytic," I hasten to add that the topic of death is not to be *introduced* by the analyst. It is to be *unmasked* since its derivatives are invariably present in the patient's material. Approached this way, the exploration of the patient's feelings about his "impending" (remember: it is *always* impending) death becomes a legitimate activity for the clinical dyad to undertake. Any extraordinary affect (e.g., excessive fear, undue longing), attitude (e.g., denial of death via counterphobic flirtations with danger), or fantasy (e.g., death as a lover) involving death would then be brought up for associative elaboration, introspection, and gaining a deeper understanding of its origins and purposes. In other words, the indirect and disguised appearance of death in patients' associations would be "translated upwards" into the language of consciousness and mutual understanding.

This, of course, is not needed when patients talk overtly of killing themselves. The analyst listening to a patient talk about suicide must maintain an attitude of equanimity, non-judgmental seriousness, and patience. This strengthens the boundary between thought and action. It is important to remember that the patient needs to extrude the forces that threaten his existence from within. With the dreaded agenda out in the open, there is a diminution of shame and sense of aloneness. Dynamic exploration then becomes possible. When matters begin to get out of hand, however, the analyst has to depart from neutrality and undertake responsible and protective action.

While management of overtly suicidal patients has received considerable attention, the subtler ways in which patients attempt to hasten their exit from this world have mostly remained unaddressed. This, however, does not mean that there are no technical dilemmas in this realm. Indeed, there are. For instance, how actively should an analyst intervene with a patient who does little exercise, is overweight, and smokes cigarettes? And, should the analyst ask if, during the course of an eight-year analysis, the analysand has ever had a physical examination? What are the pros and cons of such interventions? Does the analyst's expressed interest in such matters constitute a countertransference enactment or does it simply show a concern for the patient as well as for the analytic process itself? Doesn't ignoring the patient's subtle self-destructive behaviors permit a pocket of masochism to remain unanalyzed? Clearly, more thought is needed here.

As the exploration of the patient's feelings and attitudes about his or her death proceeds, three special aspects come to attention: (a) fantasies and actual decisions about the disposal of his or her body, (b) anticipation of parting from cherished possessions and the planning required for their dispersal, and, (c) participation in one's posthumous survival in the form of the legacy left behind. Each of these realms requires exploration. Helping the patient talk about their funeral and burial or cremation often yields rich information about their internal object relations with both their ancestors and the coming generations. For instance, one patient felt that he should be buried because it made him feel similar to his parents who had been buried *and* because he desired his children to visit his grave after he was gone. Elaborations of these themes led to rich information about his internal life both within the transference and as it existed outside the analytic treatment. However, such interpretive work has to be put on the shelf, so to speak, when it comes to acute crises emanating from the patient receiving a truly grave diagnosis.

Clinical vignette: 17

Laura Klafter, a blond sixty-year-old widowed attorney, was in psychotherapy with me for interpersonal difficulties that had plagued her for a very long time. Estranged from her son, she felt bereft and painfully alone. As our work progressed, a disastrous event occurred. Laura was diagnosed with an especially lethal form of intestinal malignancy. The day she learned of this diagnosis, she had a scheduled appointment with me. As she sat on

> her usual chair and talked about the tragedy amid sobs and tears, I noticed that she had picked up a trinket from the nearby occasional table and was caressing it, absentmindedly, with her hand. I wondered if I should bring this to her attention but decided not to; I restrained my interpretive greed in favor of remaining available, affirmative, and attuned to her distress.

Such an attitude requires enormous patience on the analyst's part, and more importantly, a certain degree of comfort with matters of life and death. The problem is that a culturally transmitted blind spot often precludes psychoanalysts' noticing that the patients are expressing a wish to talk about their death. Analysts are more comfortable in hearing about imaginary death wishes directed at them than in patients' interest in their own actual deaths (especially when such discourse is not clinically "noisy" and dangerous in reality). When they do listen to the patients' talk of their death, they readily pathologize such interest and trace its origins to guilt and masochism. What escapes them is the ubiquitous human desire to understand death and the need for help in shedding the illusion of immortality. I therefore urge that we cultivate the conceptual freedom to think that an analysis is deficient if it reaches termination without a whisper about what awaits the patient as the final chapter of his or her life.

To arrive at such a stance, analysts would need to (a) shift their view of death as being *apart* from life to its being *a part* of life; (b) recognize that man must make peace with the inevitable fact of mortality in order to live fully and truthfully; (c) understand that fear and denial of death are mostly pathological and a calm acceptance of death is mostly healthy, and (d) work through the feelings about their own death. It is only when analysts make an earnest effort to move in this existential direction that they can help patients grasp the sham nature of their "death anxiety." In the absence of such an attitude in analysts, patients finish the treatment with a tightly protected corner of their minds where infantile omnipotence prevails in the guise of the denial of mortality.

A discussion of this sort must not be allowed to skirt the actual encounter with death. Few psychotherapists deal with patients in the last weeks, days, or hours of their lives; it appears that there is little to be achieved by psychotherapy at this point. Hulsey and Frost (1995), however, argue that psychoanalytic therapy can soothe dying patients by providing a level of understanding beyond the obvious and by helping them make more conscious choices about the experience of dying. Moore (2013), a psychoanalyst who has considerable experience with terminally ill and dying patients, also makes some very significant observations in this regard. He states:

> One might imagine that in the final stages of life, we become consumed with the body and overcome with a deep sense of anger and resentment over how it has let us down, along with frustration over how it is barely under conscious control. Yet, I have not found that to be a common experience for the dying patients I have worked with .... I suspect that death, rather than creating estrangement from the body, may create an unexpected reconciliation and an unavoidable deepening of the experience of embodiment .... Dying can also be the final opportunity to ... revel in every last moment of what it is to live in the wondrous embrace of this mortal coil. (pp. 78–79)

Incredible though it may sound, the capacity to "revel" remains till the last moment in some individuals. Here is an illustration.

Clinical vignette: 18

Laura Klafter, the cancer patient described in Clinical vignette: 17, deteriorated rapidly and, despite excellent medical care, began to die within a few months of being diagnosed with a malignancy. Toward the last two months or so, she was living in her own apartment with an around-the-clock private nurse.

Her visits to my office had been replaced by an occasional phone call or text, during one of which she requested that I come and see her in her apartment. I agreed to do so. A total of eight such visits occurred before she died. These visits were fifty minutes long, just as her therapy sessions had been, and took place in her bedroom. She was unable to come to the living room. The nurse left Laura's bedroom upon my arrival and waited patiently in the living room. I pulled up a chair and sat next to Laura's bed. We spoke to each other in a halting, tender, and respectful manner.

> One day, as I was about to leave, she told me that she had not laughed for a long time and would appreciate if I told her a joke each time before leaving. Privately recognizing that this was a defense against her sadness over her condition as well as over our parting, I nonetheless was able to see the wish to live, the wish to enjoy our togetherness, and the wish to "revel" in life, in this request.[66] I decided to accede to her desire and told her some really good jokes which she thoroughly enjoyed; she laughed aloud and seemed to perk up. My last meeting with her ended on a truly fantastic joke; perhaps, we were both agreeing with a knowing and impish wink that, in the end, life itself is a good joke.

Such intimate contact brings up the issue of the analyst's physically touching a dying patient. Now, in general, analytic work is conducted with a silent pact of "abstinence" (Freud, 1915e) which precludes physical contact between the patient and the analyst.[67] While it is hardly possible to review the considerable literature that exists on this matter, a brief citation from Celenza (2011) which eloquently sums up this position is not to be omitted.

> Psychoanalysis is the science of hermeneutics—the examination and explication of meanings. Touch is nonverbal; it is a mute action—at best, it fails to reveal meaning and at worst, obfuscates. We may contact without explicating what we intend to convey. In this sense, it is anti-analytic by itself. (pp. 170–171)

However, Celenza (2011) acknowledges that in working with dying patients, touch may be permissible, and gives a few examples of this

---

[66] Our sharing jokes had a sexual element also not only because the venue was a bedroom but also due to the fact that a joke involves the build-up of a tension and ends on the "climax" of a punchline. However, being "aim-inhibited" and occurring in the context of fast approaching death, such indulgence seemed harmless.

[67] Like other taboos, this "rule" has exceptions. Some are medically necessary (e.g., if a patient has an epileptic seizure and needs to be restrained), some are formalized (e.g., analysts' shaking patients' hands at the beginning and end of each session), still others merely civil (e.g., helping a pregnant woman get up from the couch if she is experiencing difficulty), and a few totally spontaneous (e.g., see Clinical vignette: 2 where I did a high five with a patient).

from her practice. More importantly, she elaborates upon the rationale of such "indulgence".

> I am certain that these kinds of interactions have happened with all of us. Still, the question might be asked: why would touching be permissible in this circumstance? In these final moments of life, the boundaries of analysis or therapy have rightfully collapsed. With the awareness of death approaching, we face the bareness of our beings and engage with each other in more simple, existential terms. Person-to-person, we want a moment of intimacy in an unfettered and unconstrained manner, to make contact with a person's being without deprivation in these very poignant human experiences. (p. 168)

Talking of her having touched two dying male patients, Celenza asserts that "It is inhumane to withhold a gesture of caring in dire circumstances. And, touch might be one such gesture" (p. 168). My telling jokes at the end of our last five or six sessions before my patient, Laura, died, was another.

Concluding remarks

In this chapter, I have delineated ten specific guidelines for facilitating psychic development during the course of intensive psychotherapy or psychoanalysis. I have given illustrations of each and try to link clinical practice with the underlying theory in each instance. I have emphasized that these "development-facilitating interactions" do not have to replace the customary interpretive work of psychoanalysis. Yet it is possible that the "purists" amongst us would find my suggestions to be essentially anti-analytic, though they might disguise such harshness by using euphemisms like "directive," "supportive," and "pedagogic." My rejoinder to such objection is that it is hardly a matter of either–or; analytics work contains both supportive and interpretive measures. The former stabilizes the patient's ego and the latter makes that ego expose more of its instinctual, primary process underbelly. Settlage (1992) has put this balance of interactional dynamics in a most eloquent manner:

> With each undoing of some aspect of pathology, there is an opportunity for development in the same area. With each increment of development, the personality structure is strengthened. The strengthened structure increases the patient's tolerance for the therapeutic exposure of the repressed ... further therapeutic work is followed by more development, and so on. (p. 355)

Settlage's stance is supported by Killingmo's (1989) delineation of the credulous listening-affirmative intervention and skeptical listening-interpretive interaction sequence. He reminds us that the "analyst has to be in a state of constant receptivity to oscillate between the two strategic positions" (p. 77). Validating and explanatory remarks must be sprinkled between incisive and deciphering comments on the analyst's part.

Fascinatingly, two opposing camps find such an admixture disagreeable. One is the "classical" group which might derive the supportive element of the technique proposed in this chapter. The other, curiously, is composed of the analysts (Grossmark, 2018; Kohut, 1977; Schwaber, 1983, 1998) who argue that interpretation is unnecessary, if not indicating violence toward the patient's mind. To this latter group, understanding the patient and demonstrating to the patient that he or she has been understood is sufficient; layers of psychic material will automatically be revealed by the now deeply trusting patient and steps toward greater authenticity, self-confidence, and maturity will follow. To reiterate, one group (the "classical" analysts) might object to the supportive element and the other (the "postmodern" constructivists) might object to the interpretive element in my therapeutic technique.

For sorting out this conundrum, I turn to the British analyst, Kenneth Wright (1991) who speaks most convincingly of the "maternal and paternal poles of analytic technique" (p. 280). In Wright's view, analysis involves a renewal of the process of psychic formation. It provides the space within which new forms of symbols of the self may be created. However, for fully separated and representative symbols, as well as less separated and economic symbols in the human discourse to emerge, be understood, and coalesce, the analytic technique requires both maternal and paternal elements. The maternal element (holding, facilitating, enabling, and surviving) "posits faith in the background process. Things will happen if you wait" (p. 283). The paternal element (searching, confronting, deciphering, and interpreting) underlies the analyst's skepticism, his struggles with the patient's resistances, his confrontations with the turbulent world of intrapsychic conflict. Wright goes on to suggest that the two modes of intervention might be appropriate at different times and foster different modes of symbolizing. However, maternal holding of the psychically banished elements has to precede a meaningful looking at them with the aim of further self-understanding. "Containing holding" is a prior condition for "transformative looking" (p. 300). Moreover, the maternal and paternal elements of technique "provide a point and counterpoint in analysis between two styles and two visions and neither wins the day completely" (p. 280). It should also be remembered that such "maternal" and "paternal" attributes are not gender-based in a literal sense. There are male analysts who seem more "maternal" and female analysts who seem more "paternal" in technique.

Clinicians who conduct what I call "motherless psychoanalysis" rely strictly on spoken words, put a premium on interpretation, and regard ego-supportive measures as harmful "gratifications." Clinicians who conduct "fatherless" psychoanalysis, in my phraseology, consider nonverbal mutuality as the main therapeutic agent, dismiss interpretation, and are likely to see developmental interventions as integral to "unobtrusive psychoanalytic companioning" (Grossmark, 2018). Neither group is comfortable with the technique that combines development facilitation *and* interpretive unmasking, a technique that is neither "motherless" nor "fatherless."

One final point: I wish to emphasize that the equation of development work with "maternal" and an interpretive approach with "paternal" poles has its limitations. Mother also informs the child of his or her drive interests and their myriad disguises. And, father plays a role in development by unshackling the child from his symbolic tie to his mother, enlarging contact with external reality, helping modulate aggression, and laying down the law of limits and prohibitions. Both parents play a role in development. To paraphrase the African proverb, "It takes a village to raise a child" (popularized in the United States by Hillary Clinton), one could say that "It takes two parents to raise a child." And, to extend that phrase, "It takes two analysts to treat a patient": the "motherless analysis" of our profession's early days is as ineffective, in my opinion, as the "fatherless analysis" advocated by some fashionable analysts today.

Epilogue

CHAPTER FIVE

The post-self

The term "post-self" was coined by renowned American thanatologist Edwin Shneidman (1918–2009). According to him, all individuals entertain notions about what might happen to them after death. Putting religious ideas such as heaven and hell, karmic cycles of existence, and reincarnation aside, Shneidman focused upon what individuals think their "participation" in the world might be like when they are absent from it. In this context he introduced the concept of "post-self." This "refers to the ways in which one might live on, survive, or have some measure of impact or influence after the event of [one's] physical death—for instance, through one's children or through one's published works" (2008, p. 121).[68] Shneidman offered many excerpts from the novels of Herman Melville (1819–1851) to illustrate what he meant by "post-self," since Melville seemed preoccupied with the desire to be

[68] Published works are but one form of legacy one may leave behind. Other creative products (e.g., painting, sculpture), money, collections, medals, books, and civic or military decorations are among other myriad ways a "post-self" is created and sustained.

remembered after his passing. These excerpts are impressive, but more striking is the following passage from a personal letter of the novelist:

> All ambitious authors should have ghosts capable of revisiting the world, to snuff up the steam of adulation, which begins to rise straight away as the sexton throws his last shovelful on him—Down goes his body and up flies his name. (Letter to Evert Duykinck, April 5, 1849, cited in Shneidman, 1999, p. 121)

A more recent and eloquent, if ironic, portrait of one who is preoccupied with his "post-self" is provided by the philosophically inclined psychoanalyst Allen Wheelis (1975).

> I do not use myself up in living. A part of myself I save, like a miser, hoping to transmute it into something that will go on living for me in the future. With the quick I have little to do; the eminent dead are my models, the yet unborn my legatees. I am a time-binder, obsessed with mortality, spend my life creating an effigy to outlast me. In the graveyard, ceaselessly, I carve at my epitaph, trying to make it something so beautiful, so compact of meaning, that people will come from afar to read. (p. 53)

Most patients are neither so facile with words nor as consumed by their yearning for a "beautiful" post-self as Wheelis' protagonist is. In fact, there is a broad range of intensity with which people handle this matter. Some individuals pay little attention to what happens to them after their death; a multiplicity of factors underlies such indifference: denial of death, narcissistic inability to think of those left behind and/or a pollyannaish overestimation of the bereaved's fair-mindedness in sharing what property is left behind. Others plan ahead for their funeral, often going to great pains in sorting out the details. Some never think of their epitaphs, if they are going to be buried, while others write their own (Akhtar, 2011b). Some leave explicit directions about how their cremated remains are to be disposed. Others do not. Prince Philip (1921–2021) of England, for instance, labored for sixteen years in perfecting the Land Rover he wanted to be his hearse.

Then there are decisions involving the disposal of one's material possessions and money. Powerful affects and fantasies regarding separation and loss may get activated and have to be tactfully dealt with. In older and affluent patients especially the need and wished-for scenarios involving the writing of a will and deciding the fate of one's personal property warrant addressing.[69] Omission of such inquiry betrays a collusive avoidance of omnipotent defenses on the analyst's part. Inclusion of such themes, in contrast, creates the possibility for the patient to exert a modicum of control over the "shape" and emotional hues of their post-self. The point is neither to idealize the laborious assembly of credentials for a glowing obituary nor to devalue the desire to leave a little trace of the self behind one's death. The point is to help the patient see that the realm of post-self does exist and one can, consciously or unconsciously, impact upon it.

Clinical vignette: 19

Jim Hartly, a sixty-two-year-old divorced and lonely car salesman, was diagnosed with cancer of the ascending colon which rapidly spread to his liver. An abnormally situated hepatic artery precluded the much-needed infusion of appropriate medications into his liver and the ongoing chemotherapy for colon cancer failed to keep him going. His condition deteriorated rapidly and soon he was facing imminent death.

In his psychotherapy, Jim expressed intense anger and disappointment with his only child, Bobby, a thirty-year-old son who was estranged from him. Their "relationship" was replete with mutual blame, mistrust, and bitterness ever since Jim's divorce from Bobby's mother. During one particular session, Jim declared that he had decided to cut Bobby out of his will and leave all his assets to his nephew who had been very tender and caring toward him during his illness. When I asked him to elaborate on this decision, Jim retorted: "Don't you think I have a right to take revenge? Bobby has treated me so badly, why can't I do the same? You don't want me to have even that much self-respect?"

[69] The societal "respect" for a will, however, varies from culture to culture.

> I responded, "Of course, you have a right to take revenge, and a right to do whatever you see fit with your assets. However, there are two issues that you seem to have not considered: one, what if you regretted this decision as you took your last breath? And, two, after your death, do you want to be remembered by your extended family as the man who ostracized his son and left not even a penny to him in his will?" I added that "These kinds of things often find a way in long-lasting family lore, you know." Jim became pensive, and a few sessions later, informed me that he had decided to leave a small proportion to his son, leaving the far greater chunk to his nephew. He seemed satisfied and peaceful with this decision.[70]

Intervening the way I did contains, unconsciously (since only later self-reflection made me aware of it), my own earlier proposal of "good enough revenge" (Akhtar, 2014b). This essentially refers to an act of counter aggression that (i) is done just once, (ii) does not contain self-harm, (iii) is felt more in fantasy and expressed less in action, and (iv) has elements of sublimation and ego growth. While helping transform my patients fuming rage into a "good enough revenge," my eyes were on the ultimate benefits to the formation of the post-self.

Leaving material bequests is, however, not the only way people continue to live in the minds of those left behind, especially the younger generation. Erikson's (1950b) concept of "generativity" and Tähkä's (1993) description of the experience of "tenderness" also come into play here. The former subsumes the benevolent facilitation of the younger generation's growth and the latter refers to the empathetic sharing of the other's pleasure and subsequent leaving of such pleasure for them. The two attributes do not have to end with one's physical death. Generativity and tenderness toward those left behind and even the future generations to come can impart a salutary texture to the post-self one envisions for oneself. Material and psychic miserliness has to be given up and a positive mark has to be left.

---

[70] Years later, I learnt that my "advice" was legally good as well since being completely omitted from a parent's will facilitates the offspring's claiming that the former was demented and "forgot" the offspring's existence. This opens up a huge can of worms, resulting in complex legal suits.

If that mark has sonorous echoes of hardship, sacrifice, and suffering on behalf of others, that is fine too until the time such "inheritance" avoids the pitfall of last ditch sadomasochism and retains love and care for others. A couplet by the renowned Urdu poet and my father, Jan Nisar Akhtar (1915–1976), captures this sentiment in its finest detail:

> Lahoo ki booNd bhi KaNtoN pe kum nahiN hoti/
> Koi chiragh to sehra meiN chodte jaao. (1975, p. 32)[71]

[71] A rough translation which, I fear, shall rob the verses of the prosodic quality and emotional power, would go like this: "A red, shining drop of blood on the tip of this thorn is no ordinary matter/Leave—do leave—a brightly lit candle for those who are destined to cross this desert after you."

References

Abelin, E. (1971). The role of father in the separation-individuation process. In: J. B. McDevitt & C. F. Settlage (Eds.), *Separation-Individuation* (pp. 229–252). New York: International Universities Press.

Abraham, K. (1913). Some remarks on the role of grandparents in the psychology of neuroses. In: *Clinical Papers and Essays on Psychoanalysis* (pp. 44–47). New York: Brunner/Mazel, 1955.

Abraham, K. (1924a). The influence of oral eroticism on character formation. In: *Selected Papers of Karl Abraham, M.D.* (pp. 393–406). New York: Brunner/Mazel.

Abraham, K. (1924b). A short study of the development of the libido, viewed in the light of mental disorders. In: *Selected Papers on Psychoanalysis* (pp. 418–501). New York: Brunner/Mazel, 1955.

Abrams, S. (1978). The teaching and learning of psychoanalytic developmental psychology. *Journal of the American Psychoanalytic Association, 26*: 387–406.

Ainslie, R. (1997). *The Psychology of Twinship*. Northvale, NJ: Jason Aronson.

Ainsworth, M. (1967). *Infancy in Uganda: Infant Care and the Growth of Love*. Baltimore, MD: Johns Hopkins University Press.

Ainsworth, M. (1989). Attachments beyond infancy. *American Psychologist, 44*: 709–716.

Akhtar, J. N. (1975). *Pichhle Pehar*. New Delhi: Maktaba Jamia, p. 32.

Akhtar, S. (1992). Tethers, orbits, and invisible fences: clinical, developmental, sociocultural, and technical aspects of optimal distance. In: S. Kramer & S. Akhtar (Eds.), *When the Body Speaks: Psychological Meanings in Kinetic Clues* (pp. 21–57). Northvale, NJ: Jason Aronson.

Akhtar, S. (1995). A third individuation: immigration, identity, and the psychoanalytic process. *Journal of the American Psychoanalytic Association, 43*: 1051–1084.

Akhtar, S. (1996). "Someday ..." and "if only ..." fantasies: pathological optimism and inordinate nostalgia as related forms of idealization. *Journal of the American Psychoanalytic Association, 44*: 723–753.

Akhtar, S. (1998). From simplicity through contradiction to paradox: the evolving psychic reality of the borderline patient in treatment. *International Journal of Psychoanalysis, 79*: 241–252.

Akhtar, S. (1999a). *Immigration and Identity: Turmoil, Treatment, and Transformation*. Northvale, NJ: Jason Aronson.

Akhtar, S. (1999b). The distinction between needs and wishes: implications for psychoanalytic theory and technique. *Journal of the American Psychoanalytic Association, 47*: 113–151.

Akhtar, S. (2000). The shy narcissist. In: J. Sandler, R. Michels, & P. Fonagy (Eds.), *Changing Ideas in a Changing World: Essays in Honor of Arnold Cooper* (pp. 111–119). London: Karnac.

Akhtar, S. (2003a). Mentor: a developmental object of young adulthood. In: R. S. Murthy (Ed.), *Mental Health in India 1950–2000: Essays in Honor of Professor N. N. Wig* (pp. 2–8). Bangalore, India: PAHN, 2001.

Akhtar, S. (2003b). Things: developmental, psychopathological, and technical aspects of inanimate objects. *Canadian Journal of Psychoanalysis, 11*: 1–44.

Akhtar, S. (2005a). Early relationships and their internalization. In: E. Person, A. Cooper, & G. Gabbard (Eds.), *The Textbook of Psychoanalysis* (pp. 39–55). Washington, DC: American Psychiatric Press.

Akhtar, S. (Ed.) (2005b). Freud Along the Ganges: Psychoanalytic Reflections on the People and Culture of India. New York: Other Press.

Akhtar, S. (Ed.) (2008). *The Crescent and the Couch: Crosscurrents between Islam and Psychoanalysis*. Lanham, MD: Jason Aronson.

Akhtar, S. (2009a). *Comprehensive Dictionary of Psychoanalysis*. London: Karnac.

Akhtar, S. (Ed.) (2009c). *Freud and the Far East: Psychoanalytic Perspectives on the People and Culture of China, Japan, and Korea.* Lanham, MD: Jason Aronson.

Akhtar, S. (2010a). Freud's Todesangst and Ghalib's Ishrat-e-Qatra: two perspectives on death. In: S. Akhtar (Ed.), *The Wound of Mortality: Fear, Denial, and Acceptance of Death* (pp. 1–20). Lanham, MD: Jason Aronson.

Akhtar, S. (Ed.) (2010b). *The Wound of Mortality: Fear, Denial, and Acceptance of Death.* Lanham, MD: Jason Aronson.

Akhtar, S. (2011a). *Immigration and Acculturation: Mourning, Adaptation, and the Next Generation.* Lanham, MD: Jason Aronson.

Akhtar, S. (2011b). *Matters of Life and Death: Psychoanalytic Reflections.* London: Karnac.

Akhtar, S. (2012). *The African American Experience: Psychoanalytic Perspectives.* Lanham, MD: Jason Aronson.

Akhtar, S. (2013). *Psychoanalytic Listening: Methods, Limits, and Innovations.* London: Karnac.

Akhtar, S. (2014a). Mental pain of minorities. *British Journal of Psychotherapy, 30*: 36–153.

Akhtar, S. (2014b). Revenge: an overview. In: *Revenge: Narcissistic Injury, Rage, and Retaliation* (pp. 1–18). Lanham, MD: Jason Aronson.

Akhtar, S. (2015). Patience. *Psychoanalytic Review, 102*: 93–132.

Akhtar, S. (Ed.) (2016). *The New Motherhoods: Patterns of Early Child Care in Contemporary Culture.* Lanham, MD: Rowman & Littlefield.

Akhtar, S. (2018). *Mind, Culture, and Global Unrest: Psychoanalytic Reflections:* London: Routledge.

Akhtar, S. (2019). *Symptoms of Belonging.* Mt Vernon, NJ: Arseya.

Akhtar, S. (2021). *This Is What Happened* (pp. 47, 48, 64). London: Sphinx.

Akhtar, S., & Billinkoff, Z. (2011). Developmental tasks of early marriage: "Barefoot in the Park" (1967), "Raising Arizona" (1987), "The Quiet Man" (1952). *American Journal of Psychoanalysis, 71*: 110–120.

Akhtar, S., & Kanwal, G. S. (Eds.) (2017). *Bereavement: Personal Experiences and Clinical Reflections.* London: Karnac.

Akhtar, S, & Kramer, S. (Eds.) (1997). *Seasons of Life.* Northvale, NJ: Jason Aronson.

Akhtar, S., & Kramer, S. (1999). *Brothers and Sisters: Developmental, Dynamic, and Technical Aspects of the Sibling Relationship.* Northvale, NJ: Jason Aronson.

Akhtar, S., & Margery Bertoglia, S. (Eds.) (2015). *The American Latino: Psychodynamic Perspectives on Culture and Mental Health*. Lanham, MD: Jason Aronson.

Albom, M. (1998). *Tuesdays with Morrie*. New York: Bantam.

Allen, J. G., & Fonagy, P. (Eds.) (2006). *The Handbook of Mentalization-based Treatment*. Chichester, UK: John Wiley & Sons.

Allison, P. D., & Furstenberg, F. F., Jr. (1989). How marital dissolution affects children: Variations by age and sex. *Developmental Psychology, 25*: 540–559.

Amato, P. R., Spencer, L., & Booth, A. (1994). Parental divorce, marital conflict, and offspring well-being during adulthood. *Social Forum, 73*: 895–915.

Ansbacher, H., & Ansbacher, R. (1956). *The Individual Psychology of Alfred Adler*. New York: Basic Books.

Anthony, E. J. (1970). The reactions of parents to the oedipal child. In: E. J. Anthony & T. Benedek (Eds.), *Parenthood: Its Psychology and Psychopathology* (pp. 275–288). Boston, MA: Little, Brown.

Anthony, E. J., & Cohler, B. J. (1987). *The Invulnerable Child*. New York: Guilford.

Arieti, S. (1974). *Interpretation of Schizophrenia*. New York: Basic Books.

Arlow, J. A. (1961). Silence and the theory of technique. *Journal of the American Psychoanalytic Association, 9*: 44–55.

Armstrong, N. M., An, Y., Doshi, J., Erus, G., Ferrucci, L., Davatzikos, C., Deal, J. A., Lin, F. R., & Resnick, S. M. (2019). Association of midlife hearing impairment with late-life temporal lobe volume loss. *Otolaryngology–Head and Neck Surgery, 145*(9): 794–802.

Auerhahn, N., & Laub, D. (1987). Play and playfulness in Holocaust survivors. *Psychoanalytic Study of the Child, 42*: 45–58.

Balint, M. (1937). Early developmental states of the ego: primary object-love. In: *Primary Love and Psycho-Analytic Technique* (pp. 74–90). London: Hogarth, 1955.

Balint, M. (1959). *Thrills and Regressions*. London: Hogarth.

Balint, M. (1968). *The Basic Fault: Therapeutic Aspects of Regression*. London: Tavistock.

Balsam, R. (1988). On being good: the internalized sibling with examples from late adolescent analyses. *Psychoanalytic Inquiry, 8*: 66–87.

Balsam, R. (1989). Styles of connection in analysis—clinical instances. *Psychoanalytic Study of the Child, 44*: 191–198.

Balsam, R. (2000). The mother within the mother. *Psychoanalytic Quarterly, 69*: 465–492.

Baselice, K., & Thomson, J. A. (2018). Evolutionary psychology. In: S. Akhtar & S. Twemlow (Eds.), *Textbook of Applied Psychoanalysis* (pp. 81–98). London: Routledge.

Bateman A., & Fonagy, P. (2009). Randomized controlled trial of outpatient mentalization-based treatment versus structured clinical management for borderline personality disorder. *American Journal of Psychiatry, 166*(12): 1355–1364.

Beebe, B. (1986). Mother–infant mutual influence and precursors of self and object representations. In: J. Masling (Ed.), *Empirical Studies of Psychoanalytic Theories, Vol II* (pp. 27–48). Hillsdale, NJ: Lawrence Erlbaum.

Beebe, B. (2000). Co-constructing mother–infant distress. *Psychoanalytic Inquiry, 20*: 421–440.

Benedek, T. (1938). Adaptation to reality in early infancy. *Psychoanalysis Quarterly, 7*: 200–214.

Benedek, T. (1949). The psychosomatic implications of the primary unit: mother–child. *American Journal of Orthopsychiatry, 19*: 642–654.

Benedek, T. (1959). Parenthood as a development phase. *Journal of the American Psychoanalytic Association, 7*: 389–417.

Benedek, T. (1970). Fatherhood and parenthood. In: E. J. Anthony & T. Benedek (Eds.), *Parenthood: Its Psychology and Psychopathology* (pp. 169–183). Boston, MA: Little, Brown.

Benjamin, J. (1988). *The Bonds of Love: Psychoanalysis, Feminism, and the Problem of Domination*. New York: Pantheon.

Bergman, A. (1980). Ours, yours, mine. In: R. Lax, S. Bach, & J. A. Burland (Eds.), *Rapprochements: The Critical Subphase of Separation-Individuation* (pp. 199–216). New York: Jason Aronson.

Bergman, A. (2004). The experience of becoming and being a new father. In: S. Akhtar & H. Parens (Eds.), *Real and Imaginary Fathers* (pp. 107–127). Lanham, MD: Jason Aronson.

Bergman, A., & Fahey, M. F. (1999). *Ours, Yours, and Mine: Mutuality and the Emergence of the Separate Self*. Lanham, MD: Jason Aronson.

Bergmann, M. S. (1971). Psychoanalytic observations on the capacity to love. In: J. B. McDevitt and C. F. Settlage (Eds.), *Separation-Individuation* (pp. 15–40). New York: International Universities Press.

Bernstein, D. (1983). The female superego: a different perspective. *International Journal of Psychoanalysis, 64*: 187–200.

Bernstein, D. (1990). Female genital anxieties, conflicts, and typical mastery modes. *International Journal of Psychoanalysis, 71*: 151–165.

Bion, W. R. (1962). A theory of thinking. *International Journal of Psychoanalysis, 43*: 306–310.

Bion, W. R. (1965). *Transformations*. London: Karnac, 1984.

Bion, W. R. (1970). *Attention and Interpretation*. London: Karnac, 1984.

Blos, P. (1965). The initial stage of male adolescence. *Psychoanalytic Study of the Child, 20*: 145–165.

Blos, P. (1967). The second individuation process of adolescence. *Psychoanalytic Study of the Child, 22*: 162–186.

Blos, P. (1974). The genealogy of the ego ideal. *Psychoanalytic Study of the Child, 29*: 43–88.

Blos, P. (1984). Son and father. *Journal of the American Psychoanalytic Association, 32*: 301–324.

Blos, P. (1985). *Son and Father*. New York: Free Press.

Blum, H. (1996). Female psychology in progress. *Journal of the American Psychoanalytic Association, 44*: 3–9.

Blum, L. (2004). The baby as a transference object for the father. In: S. Akhtar & H. Parens (Eds.), *Real and Imaginary Fathers* (pp. 129–142). Lanham, MD: Jason Aronson.

Blum, H. (2005). The language of affect. In: S. Akhtar & H. Blum (Eds.), *The Language of Emotions: Development, Pathology, and Technique* (pp. 1–18). Lanham, MD: Jason Aronson.

Bonovitz, J. (1998). Reflections of the self in the cultural looking glass. In: S. Akhtar & S. Kramer (Eds.), *The Colors of Childhood: Separation-Individuation Across Cultural, Racial, and Ethnic Differences* (pp. 169–198). Northvale, NJ: Jason Aronson.

Borchard, D. C. (2006). *The Joy of Retirement*. New York: Amacom.

Borges, L. (1964). Limites (Limits). In: *Obra Poética 1923–1964*. Buenos Aires: Emecé.

Bornstein, B. (1951). On latency. *Psychoanalytic Study of the Child, 6*: 279–285.

Bose, G. (1921). *Concept of Repression*. Calcutta, India: Sri Gouranga.

Bowlby, J. (1956). The growth of independence in the young child. *Royal Society of Health Journal, 76*: 587–591.

Bowlby, J. (1960). Grief and mourning in infancy and early childhood. *Psychoanalytic Study of the Child, 15*: 9–52.

Bowlby, J. (1969). *Attachment and Loss, Vol. I*. New York: Basic Books.

Bowlby, J. (1973). *Attachment and Loss, Vol. II.* New York: Basic Books.

Bowlby, J. (1980). *Attachment and Loss, Vol. III.* New York: Basic Books.

Brown, C., & Lowis, M. J. (2003). Psychosocial Development in the elderly: An investigation into Erikson's ninth stage. *Journal of Aging Studies, 17*(4): 415–426.

Casement, P. (1991). *Learning from the Patient.* New York: Guilford.

Cath, S. H. (1965). Some dynamics of middle and later years: a study of depletion and restitution. In: M. A. Berezin & S. H. Cath (Eds.), *Geriatric Psychiatry: Grief, Loss, and Emotional Disorders in the Aging Process* (pp. 21–72). New York: International Universities Press.

Cath, S. H. (1966). Beyond depression, the depleted state: a study in ego psychology of the aged. *Canadian Psychiatric Association Journal, 2(Suppl.)*: 329–339.

Cath, S. H. (1982). Vicissitudes of grandparenthood: A miracle of revitalization? In: S. H. Cath, A. R. Gurwitt, & J. M. Ross (Eds.), *Father and Child: Developmental and Clinical Perspectives* (pp. 329–337). Boston, MA: Little, Brown.

Cath, S. H. (1990). The awareness of the nearness of death, depletion, and the senescent cell antigen: a reconsideration of Freud's death instinct on the new frontier between psychodynamic theory and biology. In: R. A. Nemiroff & C. A. Colarusso (Eds.), *New Dimensions in Adult Development* (pp. 420–442). New York: Basic Books.

Cath, S. H. (1997). Loss and restitution in late life. In: *The Seasons of Life: Separation-Individuation Perspectives* (pp. 127–156). Northvale, NJ: Jason Aronson.

Celenza, A. (2011). Touching the patient. In: S. Akhtar (Ed.), *Unusual Interventions: Alterations of the Frame, Method, and Relationship in Psychotherapy and Psychoanalysis* (pp. 165–176). London: Routledge.

Chasseguet-Smirgel, J. (1984). *Creativity and Perversion.* New York: W. W. Norton.

Chasseguet-Smirgel, J. (1985). *The Ego Ideal: A Psychoanalytic Essay on the Malady of the Ideal.* New York: W. W. Norton.

Chodorow, N. (1994). *Femininities, Masculinities, Sexualities.* Lexington, KY: University Press of Kentucky.

Clausen, J. (1972). The continuing problem of defining mental deficiency. *Journal of Special Education, 6*: 97–106.

Coburn, K. L., & Treeger, M. L. (1997). *Letting Go: A Parent's Guide to Understanding the College Years.* 6th edn. New York: Harper Collins, 2019.

Cohen, T., Etezady, M. H., & Pacella, B. (1993). *The Vulnerable Child, Vol. I.* Madison, CT: International Universities Press.

Cohen, T., Etezady, M. H., & Pacella, B. (1995). *The Vulnerable Child, Vol. II.* Madison, CT: International Universities Press.

Cohen, T., Etezady, M. H., & Pacella, B. (1999). *The Vulnerable Child, Vol. III.* Madison, CT: International Universities Press.

Colarusso, C. A. (1981). *Adult Development: A New Dimension in Psychodynamic Theory and Practice.* New York: Plenum.

Colarusso, C. A. (1990). The third individuation: the effect of biological parenthood on separation-individuation processes in adulthood. *Psychoanalytic Study of the Child, 45*: 170–194.

Colarusso, C. A. (1997). Separation-individuation processes in middle adulthood: The fourth individuation. In: S. Akhtar & S. Kramer (Eds.), *The Seasons of Life: Separation-Individuation Perspectives* (pp. 73–94). Northvale, NJ: Jason Aronson.

Colarusso, C. A., & Nemiroff, R. A. (1979). Some observations and hypotheses about the psychoanalytic theory of adult development. *International Journal of Psychoanalysis, 60*: 59–71.

Colarusso, C. A., & Nemiroff, R. A. (1981). *Adult Development: A New Dimension in Psychodynamic Practice.* New York: Plenum.

Colonna, A. B., & Newman, L. M. (1983). The psychoanalytic literature on siblings. *Psychoanalytic Study of the Child, 38*: 285–309.

Cooper, A. (1988). Our changing views of the therapeutic action of psychoanalysis: comparing Strachey and Loewald. *Psychoanalytic Quarterly, 57*: 15–27.

Coutts, M. (2014). *The Iceberg.* New York: Black Cat.

Darwin, C. (1838). *The Correspondence of Charles Darwin, Vol. II—1837–1843.* Cambridge: Cambridge University Press, 1986.

Dewald, P., & Schwartz, H. (1993). The life cycle of the analyst: pregnancy, illness, and disability. *Journal of the American Psychoanalytic Association, 41*: 191–207.

Didion, J. (2005). *The Year of Magical Thinking.* New York: Vintage.

Doi, T. (1962). Amae: a key concept for understanding Japanese personality structure. In: R. J. Smith & R. K. Beardsley (Eds.), *Japanese Culture: Its Development and Characteristics* (pp. 121–129). Chicago, IL: Aldine.

Doi, T. (1989). The concept of amae and its psychoanalytic implications. *International Review of Psycho-Analysis, 16*: 349–354.

Dorpat, T. L. (1976). Structural conflict and object relations conflict. *Journal of the American Psychoanalytic Association, 24*: 855–874.

Duckworth, A. (2016). *Grit: The Power of Passion and Perseverance*. New York: Charles Scribner's Sons.

Edgcumbe, R. M. (1981). Toward a developmental line for the acquisition of language. *Psychoanalytic Study of the Child, 36*: 71–103.

Edward, J., Ruskin, N., & Turrini, P. (1981). *Separation-Individuation Theory and Application*. New York: Gardener.

Eissler, K. (1976). *Sigmund Freud: His Life in Pictures and Words*. New York: Harcourt Trade, 1978.

Emde, R. N. (1980). Toward a psychoanalytic theory of affect. In: S. I. Greenspan & G. H. Pollock (Eds.), *The Course of Life: Psychoanalytic Contributions Toward Understanding Personality Development, Vol. I: Infancy and Childhood* (pp. 63–112). Rockville, MD: National Institute of Mental Health Publications.

Emde, R. N. (1981). Changing models of infancy and the nature of early development: remodeling the foundation. *Journal of the American Psychoanalytic Association, 29*: 179–219.

Emde, R. N. (1983). The pre-representational self and its affective core. *Psychoanalytic Study of the Child, 38*: 165–192.

Engel, G. (1975). The death of a twin: mourning and anniversary reactions—fragments of ten years of self analysis. *International Journal of Psychoanalysis, 56*: 23–40.

Epstein, L. (1979). Countertransference with borderline patients. In: L. Epstein & A. H. Feiner (Eds.), *Countertransference* (pp. 375–406). New York: Jason Aronson.

Erikson, E. H. (1950a). Ego psychological implications of the psychoanalytic treatment of delinquents. *Psychoanalytic Study of the Child, 6*: 97–121.

Erikson, E. H. (1950b). *Childhood and Society*. New York: W. W. Norton, 1963.

Erikson, E. H. (1956). The problem of ego identity. In: *Identity and the Life Cycle* (pp. 104–164). New York: International Universities Press, 1959.

Erikson, E. H. (1958). *Young Man Luther: A Study in Psychoanalysis and History*. New York: W. W. Norton.

Erikson, E. H. (1959). *Identity and the Life Cycle*. New York: International Universities Press.

Erikson, E. H. (1975). *Life History and the Historical Moment*. New York: W. W. Norton.

Erikson, E. H. (1982). *The Life Cycle Completed: A Review*. New York: W. W. Norton.

Erikson, E. H., & Erikson, J. M. (1998). *The Life Cycle Completed: Extended Version*. New York: W. W. Norton.

Escoll, P. (1992). Vicissitudes of optimal distance through the life cycle. In: S. Kramer & S. Akhtar (Eds.), *When the Body Speaks: Psychological Meanings in Kinetic Clues* (pp. 59–87). Northvale, NJ: Jason Aronson.

Etchegoyen, R. H. (1999). *Fundamentals of Psychoanalytic Technique*. London: Karnac.

Etezady, M. H. (1995). Narcissism: primary-secondary, fundamental, or obsolete? In: T. B. Cohen, M. H. Etezady, & B. L. Pacella (Eds.), *The Vulnerable Child, Volume 2* (pp. 3–9). Madison, CT: International Universities Press.

Etezady, M. H. (2008). Faith and the couch: a perspective on transformation. *Psychoanalytic Inquiry, 28*: 560–569.

Fairbairn, W. R. D. (1952). *An Object Relations Theory of Psychoanalysis*. New York: Basic Books.

Fallon, T., & Sherkow, S. (2013). *Disordered Thought and Development: From Chaos to Organization in the Moment*. Lanham, MD: Jason Aronson.

Fenichel, O. (1945). *The Psychoanalytic Theory of Neurosis*. New York: W. W. Norton.

Ferenczi, S. (1911). On obscene words. In: E. Jones (Trans.), *Contributions to Psycho-Analysis* (pp. 112–130). Boston, MA: Richard G. Budger, 1916.

Ferenczi, S. (1925). Psychoanalysis of sexual habits. In: *Further Contributions to the Theory and Technique of Psychoanalysis* (pp. 259–297). London: Karnac, 1980.

Ferenczi, S. (1929). The unwelcome child and his death instinct. *International Journal of Psychoanalysis, 10*: 125–129.

Fischer, N., & Fischer, N. (1991). Adolescence, sex, and neurosogenesis: a clinical perspective. In: S. Akhtar & H. Parens (Eds.), *Beyond the Symbiotic Orbit: Advances in Separation Individuation Theory* (pp. 209–226). Hillsdale, NJ: Analytic Press.

Fleiss, R. (1942). The meta-psychology of the analyst. *Psychoanalytic Quarterly, 11*: 211–227.

Fonagy, P. (1998). Moments of change in psychoanalytic theory: discussion of a new theory of psychic change. *Infant Mental Health Journal, 19*: 163–171.

Fonagy, P. (1999). Memory and therapeutic action. *International Journal of Psychoanalysis, 80*: 215–233.

Fonagy, P., & Target, M. (1997). Attachment and reflective function: the role in self-organization. *Development and Psychopathology, 9*: 679–700.

Frank, J. (2016). Complex gender identifications, regulatory anxiety, and grieving: reflections on lesbian motherhood. In: S. Akhtar (Ed.), *The New Motherhoods: Patterns of Early Childcare in Contemporary Culture* (pp. 177–186). Lanham, MD: Rowman & Littlefield.

Freeman, D. M. A. (1998). Emotional refueling in development, mythology, and cosmology: the Japanese separation-individuation experience. In: S. Akhtar & S. Kramer (Eds.), *The Colors of Childhood: Separation Individuation across Cultural, Racial, and Ethnic Differences* (pp. 17–60). Northvale, NJ: Jason Aronson.

Freeman, D. M. A. (2009). Amae: East and West. In: S. Akhtar (Ed.), *Freud and the Far East: Psychoanalytic Perspectives on the People and Culture of China, Japan, and Korea* (pp. 71–88). Lanham, MD: Jason Aronson.

Freud, A. (1965). *Normality and Pathology in Childhood*. New York: International Universities Press.

Freud, A. (1981). The concept of developmental lines: their diagnostic significance. *Psychoanalytic Study of the Child, 36*: 129–136.

Freud, S. (1898a). Sexuality in the aetiology of the neuroses. *S. E., 3*: 261–285. London: Hogarth.

Freud, S. (1900a). *The Interpretation of Dreams*. *S. E., 4–5*. London: Hogarth.

Freud, S. (1905d). *Three Essays on the Theory of Sexuality*. *S. E., 7*: 135–243. London: Hogarth.

Freud, S. (1905e). Fragment of an analysis of a case of hysteria. *S. E., 7*: 1–122. London: Hogarth.

Freud, S. (1908b). Character and anal erotism. *S. E., 9*: 167–176. London: Hogarth.

Freud, S. (1909b). Analysis of a phobia in a five-year-old boy. *S. E., 10*: 1–149. London: Hogarth.

Freud, S. (1911b). Formulation on the two principles of mental functioning. *S. E., 12*: 213–226. London: Hogarth.

Freud, S. (1911c). Psycho-analytic notes on an autobiographical account of a case of paranoia. *S. E., 12*: 3–80. London: Hogarth.

Freud, S. (1912d). On the universal tendency to debasement in the sphere of love. *S. E., 11*: 178–190. London: Hogarth.

Freud, S. (1912e). Recommendations to physicians practising psycho-analysis. *S. E., 12*: 109–120. London: Hogarth.

Freud, S. (1912–13). *Totem and Taboo*. *S. E., 13*: 1–161. London: Hogarth.

Freud, S. (1913i). The disposition to obsessional neurosis. *S. E., 12*: 311–326. London: Hogarth.

Freud, S. (1914c). On narcissism: an introduction. *S. E., 14*: 69–102. London: Hogarth.

Freud, S. (1914g). Remembering, repeating and working-through. *S. E., 12*: 145–156. London: Hogarth.

Freud, S. (1915b). Thoughts for the times on war and death. *S. E., 14*: 275–300. London: Hogarth.

Freud, S. (1915d). Repression. *S. E., 14*: 146–158. London: Hogarth.

Freud, S. (1915e). The unconscious. *S. E., 14*: 159–216. London: Hogarth.

Freud, S. (1916a). On transience. *S. E., 14*: 303–307. London: Hogarth.

Freud, S. (1916d). Some character-types met with in psycho-analytic work. *S. E., 14*: 310–333. London: Hogarth.

Freud, S. (1916–17). *Introductory Lectures on Psycho-analysis*. *S. E., 15–16*: 243–463. London: Hogarth.

Freud, S. (1917e). Mourning and melancholia. *S. E., 14*: 237–258. London: Hogarth.

Freud, S. (1918b). From the history of an infantile neurosis. *S. E., 17*: 7–124. London: Hogarth.

Freud, S. (1920g). *Beyond the Pleasure Principle*. *S. E., 18*: 7–64. London: Hogarth.

Freud, S. (1921c). *Group Psychology and the Analysis of the Ego*. *S. E., 18*: 65–144. London: Hogarth.

Freud, S. (1923b). *The Ego and the Id*. *S. E., 19*: 1–66. London: Hogarth.

Freud, S. (1924d). The dissolution of the Oedipus complex. *S. E., 19*: 171–188. London: Hogarth.

Freud, S. (1925h). Negation. *S. E., 19*: 235–239. London: Hogarth.

Freud, S. (1925j). Some psychical consequences of the anatomical distinction between the sexes. *S. E., 19*: 241–258. London: Hogarth.

Freud, S. (1926d). *Inhibitions, Symptoms and Anxiety*. *S. E., 20*: 75–175. London: Hogarth.

Freud, S. (1927c). *The Future of an Illusion*. *S. E., 21*: 5–56. London: Hogarth.

Freud, S. (1929). Letter from Freud to Ludwig Binswanger, April 11. In: G. Fichtner (Ed.), *The Sigmund Freud—Ludwig Binswanger Correspondence 1908–1938* (p. 196). London: Open Gate, 2003.

Freud, S. (1930a). *Civilization and Its Discontents*. *S. E., 21*: 64–145. London: Hogarth.

Freud, S. (1933a). *New Introductory Lectures on Psycho-analysis. S. E., 22*: 7–182. London: Hogarth.

Freud, S. (1940a). *An Outline of Psycho-analysis. S. E., 23*: 139–207. London: Hogarth.

Freud, S. (1941e). Address to the members of the *B'nai B'rith. S. E., 20*: 271–274. London: Hogarth.

Freud, S. (1950a). A project for a scientific psychology. *S. E., 1*: 295–343. London: Hogarth.

Furman, E. (1974). *A Child's Parent Dies: Studies in Childhood Bereavement*. New Haven, CT: Yale University Press.

Gabbard, G. O. (1997). Challenges in the analysis of adult patients with histories of childhood sexual abuse. *Canadian Journal of Psychoanalysis, 5*: 1–25.

Garfield, R. (2004). Making a case for father hunger in girls. In: S. Akhtar & H. Parens (Eds.), *Real and Imaginary Fathers: Development, Transference, and Healing* (pp. 34–44). Northvale, NJ: Jason Aronson.

Gedo, J. E. (1997). In praise of leisure. In: C. W. Socarides & S. Kramer (Eds.), *Work and Its Inhibitions: Psychoanalytic Essays* (pp. 133–141). Madison, CT: International Universities Press.

Gibran, K. (1923). *The Prophet*. New York: Alfred A. Knopf.

Gilligan, C. (1982). *In a Different Voice: Psychological Theory and Women's Development*. Cambridge, MA: Harvard University Press.

Glazer, D. (2016). Modern families: reflections on gender identity, sexual orientation, and motherhood. In: S. Akhtar (Ed.), *The New Motherhoods: Patterns of Early Child Care in Contemporary Culture* (pp. 152–176). Lanham, MD: Rowman & Littlefield.

Glazer, D., & Drescher, J. (2001). *Gay and Lesbian Parenting*. Binghampton, NY: Haworth Medical Publishing.

Goldsmith, S. (1995). Oedipus or Orestes?: aspects of gender identity development in homosexual men. *Psychoanalytic Inquiry, 15*: 112–124.

Green, A. (1986). *On Private Madness*. London: Hogarth.

Greenacre, P. (1953). Certain relationships between fetishism and faulty development of the body image. *Psychoanalytic Study of the Child, 8*: 79–98.

Greenacre, P. (1958). Early physical determinants in the development of the sense of identity. In: *Emotional Growth: Psychoanalytic Studies of the Gifted and a Great Variety of Other Individuals* (pp. 113–127). New York: International Universities Press.

Greenacre, P. (1960). Further notes on fetishism. *Psychoanalytic Study of the Child, 15*: 191–207.

Greenberg, J. R., & Mitchell, S. A. (1983). *Object Relations in Psychoanalytic Theory*. Cambridge, MA: Harvard University Press.

Greenson, R. R. (1967). *The Technique and Practice of Psycho-analysis*. New York: International Universities Press.

Greenspan, S. I. (1980). *Intelligence and Adaptation: An Integration of Psychoanalytic and Piagetian Developmental Psychology*. New York: International Universities Press.

Greenspan, S. I. (2007a). Infant–caregiver interactions and the developmental, individual-difference, relationship-based (DIR) model: implications for psychopathology and the psychotherapeutic process. *Journal of Infant, Child and Adolescent Psychotherapy, 6*: 211–244.

Greenspan, S. I. (2007b). Levels of infant–caregiver interactions and the DIR model: implications for the development of signal affects, the regulation of mood and behavior, the formation of a sense of self, the creation of internal representation, and the construction of defenses and character structure. *Journal of Infant, Child and Adolescent Psychotherapy, 6*: 174–210.

Grossmark, R. (2018). *The Unobtrusive Relational Analyst: Explorations in Psychoanalytic Companioning*. New York: Routledge.

Grubrich-Simitis, I. (1984). From concretism to metaphor: thoughts on some theoretical and technical aspects of the psychoanalytic work with children of Holocaust survivors. *Psychoanalytic Study of the Child, 39*: 301–319.

Grunberger, B. (1989). *New Essays in Narcissism*. London: Free Association.

Gulati, R., & Pauley, D. (2019). The half embrace of psychic bisexuality. *Journal of the American Psychoanalytic Association, 67*: 97–121.

Gutmann, D. L. (1980). Psychoanalysis and aging: a developmental view. In: S. I. Greenspan & G. H. Pollock (Eds.), *Adulthood and the Aging Process* (pp. 489–517). Washington, DC: NIMH Publications.

Guttman, S. A., Jones R. L., & Parrish, S. M. (Eds.) (1980). *The Concordance to the Standard Edition of the Complete Psychological Works of Sigmund Freud*. Boston, MA: G. K. Hall.

Gu, M. D. (2006). The filial piety complex: variations on the Oedipus theme in Chinese literature and culture. *Psychoanalytic Quarterly, 75*: 163–195.

Hamilton, G. (1986). Positive projective identification. *International Journal of Psychoanalysis, 67*: 489–496.

Harley, M., & Weil, A. (1979). Introduction. In: *The Selected Papers of Margaret S. Mahler, Vol. I: Infantile Psychosis and Early Contributions* (pp. ix–xx). New York: Jason Aronson.

Harrison, A. M. (2012). Parent–child treatment: searching for a loss mother. In: S. Akhtar (Ed.), *The Mother and Her Child: Clinical Aspects of Attachment, Separation, and Loss* (pp. 79–92). Lanham, MD: Jason Aronson.

Harrison, A. M., & Beebe, B. (2018). Rhythms of dialogue in infant research and child analysis: implicit and explicit forms of therapeutic action. *Psychoanalytic Psychology, 35*: 367–381.

Harrison, Y. (2016). Mothers without motherlands. In: S. Akhtar (Ed.), *The New Motherhoods: Patterns of Early Child Care in Contemporary Culture* (pp. 145–156). Lanham, MD: Rowman & Littlefield.

Hartmann, H. (1939). *Ego Psychology and the Problem of Adaptation*. D. Rapaport (Trans.). New York: International Universities Press, 1958.

Hartmann, H. (1950). Comments on the psychoanalytic theory of the ego. In: *Essays on Ego Psychology* (pp. 113–141). New York: International Universities Press.

Hartmann, H. (1952). The mutual influences of the development of ego and id. *Psychoanalytic Study of the Child, 7*: 9–30.

Hauser, S., Allen, J., & Golden, E. (2006). *Out of the Woods: Tales of Resilient Teens*. Cambridge, MA: Harvard University Press.

Hausner, R. S. (2000). The therapeutic and working alliances. *Journal of the American Psychoanalytic Association, 48*: 155–187.

Herzog, J. (1984). Fathers and young children: fathering daughters and fathering sons. In: J. D. Call, E. Galenson, & R. Tyson (Eds.), *Foundations of Infant Psychiatry Vol. 2* (pp. 335–343). New York: Basic Books.

Herzog, J. (2001). *Father Hunger: Clinical and Developmental Explorations*. Hillsdale, NJ: Analytic Press.

Hite, S. (1976). *The Hite Report on Female Sexuality*. New York: Macmillan.

Hite, S. (1981). *The Hite Report on Men and Male Sexuality*. New York: Alfred A. Knopf.

Hoffer, A. (Ed.) (2015). *Freud and the Buddha: The Couch and the Cushion*. London: Karnac.

Hoffman, L., Johnson, E., Foster, M., & Wright, J. (2010). What happens when you die: 3–4 year olds chatting about death. In: S. Akhtar (Ed.), *The Wound of Mortality: Fear, Denial, and Acceptance of Death* (pp. 21–36). Lanham, MD: Jason Aronson.

Holmes, D. E. (2006a). The wrecking effects of race and social class on self and success. *Psychoanalytic Quarterly, 75*: 215–235.

Holmes, D. E. (2006b). Racial transference reactions in psychoanalytic treatment: an update. In: R. Moodley & S. Palmer (Eds.), *Race, Culture and Psychotherapy: Critical Perspectives in Multicultural Practice* (pp. 61–73). New York: Routledge.

Hooke, M. S., & Akhtar, S. (Eds.) (2007). *The Geography of Meanings: Psychoanalytic Perspectives on Place, Space, Land, and Dislocation*. London: International Psychoanalytical Association.

Horney, K. (1926). The flight of womanhood. *International Journal of Psychoanalysis, 7*: 324–329.

Houtzager, G. (2004). *The Complete Encyclopedia of Greek Mythology*. New York: Chartwell.

Hulsey, T. L., & Frost, C. J. (1995). Psychoanalytic psychotherapy and the tragic sense of life and death. *Bulletin of the Menninger Clinic, 59*: 145–159.

Imaginary Crimes (1994). Directed by A. Drazan, a Morgan Creek Entertainment production.

Ivey, G. (2008). Enactment controversies: a critical review of current debates. *International Journal of Psychoanalysis, 88*: 19–38.

Issacharoff, A. (1979). Barriers to knowing. In: L. Epstein & A. H. Feiner (Eds.), *Countertransference* (pp. 27–44). New York: Jason Aronson.

Iyama, A., & Inouye, T. (1992). Spindle activity in the waking EEG in older adults. *Clinical Electroencephalography, 23*: 137–141.

Jacobson, E. (1964). *The Self and the Object World*. New York: International Universities Press.

Jaques, E. (1965). Death and the mid-life crisis. *International Journal of Psychoanalysis, 46*: 458–472.

Jones, E. (1935). Early female sexuality. *International Journal of Psychoanalysis, 16*: 263–273.

Jung, C. G. (1933). *Modern Man in Search of a Soul*. New York: Houghton Mifflin Harcourt.

Kafka, J. (1989). *Multiple Realities in Clinical Practice*. New Haven, CT: Yale University Press.

Kakar, S. (1989). The maternal-feminine in Indian psychoanalysis. *International Review of Psycho-Analysis, 16*: 355–362.

Kakar, S. (2019). Last claims: sexuality and sexual imagination in old age. *Psychoanalytic Quarterly, 88*: 813–837.

Katan, A. (1961). Some thoughts about the role of verbalization in early childhood. *Psychoanalytic Study of the Child, 16*: 184–188.

Kernberg, O. F. (1967). Borderline personality organization. *Journal of the American Psychoanalytic Association, 15*: 641–685.

Kernberg, O. F. (1974a). Barriers to falling and remaining in love. *Journal of the American Psychoanalytic Association, 22*: 486–511.

Kernberg, O. F. (1974b). Mature love: prerequisites and characteristics. *Journal of the American Psychoanalytic Association, 22*: 743–768.

Kernberg, O. F. (1980). *Internal World and External Reality: Object Relations Theory Applied*. New York: Jason Aronson.

Kernberg, O. F. (1982). Self, ego, affects, and drives. *Journal of the American Psychoanalytic Association, 30*: 893–918.

Kernberg, P. F., & Richards, A. K. (1988). Siblings of preadolescents: their role in development. *Psychoanalytic Inquiry, 8*: 51–65.

Kestenberg, J. S. (1975). *Children and Parents*. New York: Jason Aronson.

Kestenberg, J. S., & Brenner, I. (1995). Narcissism in the service of survival. In: T. Cohen, M. H. Etezady, & B. Pacella (Eds.), *The Vulnerable Child, Vol. II* (pp. 35–50). Madison, CT: International Universities Press.

Khan, M. M. R. (1983a). On lying fallow. In: *Hidden Selves: Between Theory and Practice in Psychoanalysis* (pp. 183–188). New York: International Universities Press.

Khan, M. M. R. (1983b). *Hidden Selves: Between Theory and Practice in Psychoanalysis*. New York: International Universities Press.

Killingmo, B. (1989). Conflict and deficit: implications for technique. *International Journal of Psychoanalysis, 70*: 65–79.

Kinsey, A., Pomeroy, W., & Martin, C. (1948). *Sexual Behavior in the Human Male*. New York: W. B. Saunders.

Kinsey, A., Pomeroy, W., & Martin, C. (1953). *Sexual Behavior in the Human Female*. New York: W. B. Saunders.

Kleeman, J. A. (1971). The establishment of core gender identity in normal girls. *Archives of Sexual Behavior, 1*: 103–116.

Klein, G. S. (1967). Peremptory ideation: structure and force in motivated ideas. *Psychological Issues, 5*: 18–19.

Klein, M. (1927). Criminal tendencies in normal children. In: *Love, Guilt and Reparation and Other Works—1921–1945* (pp. 170–185). New York: Free Press, 1975.

Klein, M. (1932). *The Psychoanalysis of Children*. New York: Free Press, 1975.

Klein, M. (1933). The early development on conscience in the child. In: *Love, Guilt and Reparation and Other Works—1921–1945* (pp. 248–257). New York: Free Press, 1975.

Klein, M. (1935). A contribution to the psychogenesis of manic depressive states. In: *Love, Guilt and Reparation and Other Works—1921–1945* (pp. 262–289). New York: Free Press, 1975.

Klein, M. (1937). Love, guilt and reparation. In: *Love, Guilt and Reparation and Other Works—1921–1945* (pp. 306–333). New York: Free Press, 1975.

Klein, M. (1940). Mourning and its relation to manic depressive states. In: *Love, Guilt and Reparation and Other Works—1921–1945* (pp. 344–369). New York: Free Press, 1975.

Klein, M. (1945). The Oedipus complex in light of early anxieties. In: *Love, Guilt and Reparation and Other Works—1921–1945* (pp. 370–419). New York: Free Press, 1975.

Klein, M. (1957). Envy and gratitude. In: *Envy and Gratitude and Other Works—1946–1963* (pp. 176–235). New York: Free Press, 1975.

Klein, M. (1963). On the sense of loneliness. In: *Envy and Gratitude and Other Works—1946–1963* (pp. 300–313). New York: Free Press, 1975.

Kleiner, J. (1970). On nostalgia. *Bulletin of the Philadelphia Association for Psychoanalysis, 20*: 11–30.

Kohlberg, L. (1981). *The Philosophy of Moral Development: Moral Stages and the Idea of Justice*. San Francisco, CA: Harper & Row.

Kohlberg, L. (1984). *The Psychology of Moral Development: the Nature and Validity of Moral Stages*. San Francisco, CA: Harper & Row.

Kohut, H. (1971). *The Analysis of the Self*. New York: International Universities Press.

Kohut, H. (1977). *The Restoration of the Self*. New York: International Universities Press.

Kramer, S. (1987). A contribution to the concept "the exception" as a developmental phenomenon. *Child Abuse and Neglect, 11*: 367–370.

Kramer, S. (1998). Some vicissitudes of child-rearing. In: S. Akhtar & S. Kramer (Eds.), *The Colors of Childhood: Separation-Individuation Across Cultural, Racial, and Ethnic Differences* (pp. 1–15). Northvale, NJ: Jason Aronson.

Kramer, S., Byerly, L., & Akhtar, S. (1997). Growing together, growing apart, growing up, and growing down. In: S. Akhtar & S. Kramer (Eds.), *The Seasons of Life: Separation-Individuation Perspectives* (pp. 1–22). Northvale, NJ: Jason Aronson.

Kris, A. O. (1996). *Free Association: Method and Process*. London: Karnac.

Kulish, N., & Holtzman, D. (1998). Persephone, the loss of virginity, and the female oedipal complex. *International Journal of Psychoanalysis, 79*: 57–71.

Lacayo, R. (1984). Meeting of two masters: Sir David Lean and Lord Snowdon take aim at "A Passage to India". *Time*, August 27: 54–55.

Lachman, M. (2004). Development in midlife. *Annual Review of Psychology, 55*: 305–331.

Laplanche, J., & Pontalis, J.-B. (1973). *The Language of Psychoanalysis*. D. Nicholson-Smith (Trans.). New York: W. W. Norton.

Lax, R. F. (2008). Becoming really old: the indignities. *Psychoanalytic Quarterly, 77*: 835–857.

Leave No Trace (2018). Directed by D, Granik, a BRON Studios production.

Levine, H. (1997). Men at work: work ego and identity in analysis for development. In: C. W. Socarides & S. Kramer (Eds.), *Work and Its Inhibitions: Psychoanalytic Essays* (pp. 143–157). Madison, CT: International Universities Press.

Le Goués, G. (2006). Tendresse et dignité au cours du viellissemeint. In: R. Perron, *Psychanalystes, qui êtes-vous?* Paris: Interéditions.

Levinson, N. (2003). Panel on acting out and/or enactment. *International Journal of Psychoanalysis, 84*: 151–155.

Levinson, D., Darrow, C., Klein, E., Levinson, M., & McKee, B. (1978). *The Seasons of a Man's Life*. New York: Alfred A. Knopf.

Lichtenberg, J. (1982). Reflections on the first year of life. *Psychoanalytic Inquiry, 1*: 695–730.

Lichtenberg, J. (1983). *Psychoanalysis and Infant Research: Psychoanalytic Inquiry*. New York: Analytic Press.

Lichtenstein, H. (1963). The dilemma of human identity: notes on self-transformation, self-objectivation, and metamorphosis. *Journal of the American Psychoanalytic Association, 11*: 173–223.

Lidz, T. (1968). *The Person: His and Her Development throughout the Life Cycle*. New York: Basic Books, 1983.

Litowitz, B. (1998). An expanded developmental line for negation: rejection, refusal, denial. *Journal of the American Psychoanalytic Association, 46*: 121–148.

Livingston, R. (2017). Death of a spouse. In: S. Akhtar & G. S. Kanwal (Eds.), *Bereavement: Personal Experiences and Clinical Reflections* (pp. 97–116). London: Karnac.

Loewald, H. W. (1951). Ego and reality. *International Journal of Psychoanalysis, 32*: 10–21.

Loewald, H. W. (1960). On the therapeutic action of psychoanalysis. *Journal of the American Psychoanalytic Association, 41*: 16–33.

Loewald, H. W. (1971). On motivation, and instinct theory. *Psychoanalytic Study of the Child, 26*: 91–128.

Loewald, H. W. (1973). Comments on some instinctual manifestations of superego formation. *Annals of Psychoanalysis, 1*: 104–116.

Loewald, H. W. (1979). The waning of the Oedipus complex. *Journal of the American Psychoanalytic Association, 27*: 751–775.

Lowy, F. (2017). Death of sibling. In: S. Akhtar & G. S. Kanwal (Eds.), *Bereavement: Personal Experiences and Clinical Reflections* (pp. 83–95). London: Karnac.

Ma, H. K. (2013). The moral development of the child: an integrated model. www.frontiersin.org/13november2013. Accessed June 10, 2019.

Madow, L. (1997). On the way to a second symbiosis. In: S. Akhtar & S. Kramer (Eds.), *The Seasons of Life: Separation-Individuation Perspectives* (pp. 157–170). Northvale, NJ: Jason Aronson.

Mahler, M. S. (1967). On human symbiosis and the vicissitudes of individuation. *Journal of the American Psychoanalytic Association, 15*: 740–763.

Mahler, M. S. (1970). *On Human Symbiosis and the Vicissitudes of Individuation. Volume II: Separation-Individuation*. New York: Basic Books.

Mahler, M. S. (1972). Rapprochement subphase of the separation-individuation process. In: *The Selected Papers of Margaret S. Mahler, Vol. 2* (pp. 131–148). New York: Jason Aronson.

Mahler, M. S. (1974). Symbiosis and individuation: the psychological birth of the human infant. In: *The Selected Papers of Margaret S. Mahler, Volume 2* (pp. 149–165). New York: Jason Aronson, 1979.

Mahler, M. S., Pine, F., & Bergman, A. (1975). *The Psychological Birth of the Human Infant: Symbiosis and Individuation*. New York: Basic Books.

Mamdani, M. (2004). *Good Muslim, Bad Muslim*. New York: Doubleday.

Margolis, G. (1966). Secrecy and identity. *International Review of Psycho-Analysis, 47*: 517–522.

Margolis, G. (1974). The psychology of keeping secrets. *International Journal of Psychoanalysis, 1*: 291–296.

Masters, W. H., & Johnson, V. E. (1966). *Human Sexual Response*. New York: Bantam.

Masters, W. H., & Johnson, V. E. (1970). Human Sexual Inadequacy. New York: Bantam.

Masur, C. (2001). Can women mourn their mothers? In: S. Akhtar (Ed.), *The Three Faces of Mourning: Melancholia, Manic Defense, and Moving On* (pp. 34–45). Northvale, NJ: Jason Aronson.

May, R. (1950). *The Meaning of Anxiety*. New York: W. W. Norton, 1996.

McDonald, M. (1970). *Not by the Color of Their Skin*. New York: International Universities Press.

McLaughlin, J. T. (1996). Through the patient's looking-glass: reflections upon the analyst's self-inquiry. *Canadian Journal of Psychoanalysis, 4*: 205–229.

Meyers, H. (2001). Does mourning become Electra? Oedipal and separation-individuation issues in a woman's loss of her mother. In: S. Akhtar (Ed.), *The Three Faces of Mourning: Melancholia, Manic Defense, and Moving On* (pp. 13–31). Northvale, NJ: Jason Aronson.

Money, J. (1955). Hermaphroditism, gender and precocity in hyperadrenocorticism: psychologic findings. *Bulletin of Johns Hopkins Hospital, 96*: 253–264.

Money, J., & Ehrhardt, A. (1972). *Man, Woman, Boy, and Girl*. Baltimore, MD: Johns Hopkins University Press.

Moore, M. (2013). When the body betrays. In: S. Akhtar (Ed.), *Betrayal: Developmental, Literary, and Clinical Realms* (pp. 61–80). London: Karnac.

Music Box (1989). Directed by Costa-Gravas, a Carolco production.

Musick, K., & Meier, A. (2010). Are both parents better than one? *Social Science Research, 39*: 814–830.

My Girl (1991). Directed by H. Zieff, a Columbia Pictures production.

Nagy, M. (1948). The child's theories concerning death. *Journal of Genetic Psychology, 73*: 3–27.

Nemiah, J. C., & Sifneos, P. E. (1970). *Modern Trends in Psychosomatic Medicine. Volume Two.* London: Butterworth.

Neubauer, P. B. (1983). The importance of the sibling experience. *Psychoanalytic Study of the Child, 38*: 325–336.

Niederland, W. (1968). Clinical observations on the "survivor syndrome". *International Journal of Psychoanalysis, 49*: 313–315.

Notman, M. T. (2014). Reflections on widowhood and its effects on the self. *Psychodynamic Psychiatry, 42*: 65–88.

Novick, J., & Novick, K. K. (2002). Two systems of self-regulation. *Journal of Psychoanalytic Social Work, 8*: 95–122.

Novick, J., & Novick, K. K. (2019). What we can learn about confidentiality from children and adolescents. In: S. Akhtar & A. Abbasi (Eds.), *Privacy: Developmental, Cultural, and Clinical Realms* (pp. 46–56). London: Routledge.

Ogden, T. (1994). *Subjects of Analysis*. Northvale, NJ: Jason Aronson.

Oldham, J. M. (1989). The third individuation: Middle-aged children and their parents. In: J. M. Oldham & R. S. Liebert (Eds.), *The Middle Years: New Psychoanalytic Perspectives* (pp. 89–104). New Haven, CT: Yale University Press.

Olinick, S. (1976). Parallel analyzing functions in work ego and observing ego. *Journal of the Philadelphia Association for Psychoanalysis, 3*: 3–21.

O'Neil, M. K. (2016). Single mothers and women's autonomy. In: S. Akhtar (Ed.), *The New Motherhoods: Patterns of Early Child Care in Contemporary Culture* (pp. 51–66). Lanham, MD: Rowman & Littlefield.

Parens, H. (1975). Parenthood as a developmental phase. *Journal of the American Psychoanalytic Association, 23*: 154–165.

Parens, H. (1988). Siblings in early childhood: some direct observational findings. *Psychoanalytic Inquiry, 8*: 31–50.

Parens, H. (2016). The changing morphology of parenthood: its implications for separation-individuation theory. In: S. Akhtar (Ed.), *The New Motherhoods: Patterns of Early Child Care in Contemporary Culture* (pp. 15–40). Lanham, MD: Rowman & Littlefield.

Parens, H., Blum, H. P., & Akhtar, S. (Eds.) (2008). *The Unbroken Soul: Tragedy, Trauma, and Resilience*. Lanham, MD: Jason Aronson.

Parens, H., Pollock, L., Stern, J., & Kramer, S. (1976). On the girl's entry into the Oedipus complex. *Journal of the American Psychoanalytic Association, 24S*: 79–107.

Piaget, J. (1932). *The Moral Judgement of the Child*. London: Penguin, 1977.

Piaget, J. (1937). *The Construction of Reality in the Child*. New York: Basic Books.

Piaget, J. (1963). *The Psychology of Intelligence*. London: Routledge, 2001.

Pierce, C. (1970). Offensive mechanisms. In: F. B. Barbour (Ed.), *The Black Seventies* (pp. 265–282). Boston, MA: Porter Sargent.

Pine, F. (1979). On the pathology of the separation-individuation process as manifested in later clinical work: An attempt at delineation. *International Journal of Psychoanalysis, 60*: 225–242.

Pine, F. (1987). *Developmental Theory and Clinical Process*. New Haven, CT: Yale University Press.

Pine, F. (1988). The four psychologies of psychoanalysis and their place in clinical work. *Journal of the American Psychoanalytic Association, 36*: 571–596.

Pine, F. (1997). *Diversity and Direction in Psychoanalytic Technique*. New Haven, CT: Yale University Press.

Pine, F. (1998). *Diversity and Direction in Psychoanalytic Technique*. New Haven, CT: Yale University Press.

Piontelli, A. (1987). Infant observation from before birth. *International Journal of Psychoanalysis,* 68: 453–463.

Piontelli, A. (1988). A prenatal life reflected in the analysis of a psychotic girl at age two. *International Review of Psycho-Analysis, 15*: 73–81.

Piontelli, A. (1992). *From Fetus to Child: An Observational and Psychoanalytic Study*. New York: Tavistock/Routledge.

Ployé, P. (2006). *The Prenatal Theme in Psychotherapy*. London: Karnac.

Poznanski, E. D. (1972). The "replacement child": a saga of unresolved parental grief. *Journal of Pediatrics, 81*: 1190–1193.

Provence, S., & Solnit, A. J. (1983). Development-promoting aspects of the sibling experience. *Psychoanalytic Study of the Child, 38*: 337–351.

Pruett, K. (1988). *The Nurturing Father*. New York: Warner.

Quinodoz, J. M. (2008). *Listening to Hanna Segal: Her Contribution to Psychoanalysis*. London: Routledge.

Quinodoz, J. M. (2010). How translations of Freud's writings have influenced French psychoanalytic thinking. *International Journal of Psychoanalysis, 91*: 695–716.

Rangell, L. (1963). The scope of intrapsychic conflict: microscopic and macroscopic considerations. *Psychoanalytic Study of the Child, 18*: 75–102.

Riese, M. L. (1990). Neonatal temperament in monozygotic and dizygotic twins. *Child Development, 6*: 1230–1237.

Roland, A. (1988). *In Search of the Self in India and Japan*. Princeton, NJ: Princeton University Press.

Roland, A. (1996). *Cultural Pluralism and Psychoanalysis: The Asian and North American Experience*. New York: Routledge.

Ross, J. M. (1975). The development of paternal identity: a critical review of the literature on nurturance and generativity in boys and men. *Journal of the American Psychoanalytic Association, 23*: 783–817.

Ross, J. M. (1977). Towards fatherhood: the epigenesis of paternal identity during a boy's first decade. *International Review of Psycho-Analysis, 4*: 327–347.

Ross, J. M. (1990). The eye of the beholder: on the developmental dialogue between fathers and daughters. In: R. A. Nemiroff & C. A. Colarusso (Eds.), *New Dimensions in Adult Development* (pp. 47–72). New York: Basic Books.

Ross, J. M. (1994). *What Men Want*. Cambridge, MA: Harvard University Press.

Roughton, R. (2002). Rethinking homosexuality: what it teaches us about psychoanalysis. *Journal of the American Psychoanalytic Association, 50*: 733–763.

Rubin, J. (2005). Psychoanalytic and Buddhist history and theory. In: S. Akhtar (Ed.), *Freud Along the Ganges: Psychoanalytic Reflections on the People and Culture of India* (pp. 335–358). New York: Other Press.

Sabbadini, A. (1992). Listening to silence. *Scandinavian Psychoanalytic Review, 15*: 27–36.

Sander, L. W. (1962). Issues in early mother–child interaction. *Journal of the American Academy of Child Psychiatry, 1*: 141–166.

Sander, L. W. (1988). The event-structure of regulation in the neonate-caregiver system as a biological background for early organization of psychic structure. *Progress in Self Psychology, 3*: 64–67.

Sandler, J. (1960). The background of safety. *International Journal of Psychoanalysis, 41*: 352–363.

Sandler, J. (1962). The Hampstead Index as an instrument of psychoanalytic research. *International Journal of Psychoanalysis, 43*: 287–291.

Sandler, J., & Sandler, A.-M. (1998). *Internal Objects Revisited*. London: Karnac.

Sarnoff, C. (1976). *Latency*. New York: Jason Aronson.

Saudino, K. J., Cherny, S. S., & Plomin, R. (2000) Parent ratings of temperament in twins. *Twin Research, 3*: 224–233.

Schafer, R. (1976). *A New Language for Psychoanalysis*. New Haven, CT: Yale University Press.

Schafer, R. (1983). *The Analytic Attitude*. New York: Basic Books.

Schlesinger, H. (2003). *The Texture of Treatment: On the Matter of Psychoanalytic Technique*. Hillsdale, NJ: Analytic Press.

Schopenhauer, A. (1851). Über die anscheinende Absichtlichkeit im Schicksale des Einzelnen. *Parerga and Paralipomena, 1*. In: *Sämtliche Werke*. Leipzig, Germany: Hubscher, 1938.

Schwaber, E. (1983). Psychoanalytic listening and psychic reality. *International Review of Psycho-Analysis, 10*: 379–392.

Schwaber, E. (1998). From whose point of view? A neglected question in analytic listening. *Psychoanalytic Quarterly, 67*: 645–661.

Searles, H. F. (1960). *The Non-Human Environment in Normal Development and in Schizophrenia*. New York: International Universities Press.

Segal, H. (1958). Fear of death—notes on the analysis of an old man. *International Journal of Psychoanalysis, 39*: 178–181.

Settlage, C. F. (1992). Psychoanalytic observations on adult development in life and in the therapeutic relationship. *Psychoanalytic Contemporary Thought, 15*: 349–374.

Settlage, C. F. (1993). Therapeutic process and developmental process in the restructuring of object and self-constancy. *Journal of the American Psychoanalytic Association, 41*: 473–492.

Settlage, C. F. (1994). On the contribution of separation-individuation theory to psychoanalysis: developmental process, pathogenesis, therapeutic process and technique. In: S. Kramer & S. Akhtar (Eds.), *Mahler and Kohut: Perspectives on Development, Psychopathology, and Technique* (pp. 17–52). Northvale, NJ: Jason Aronson.

Settlage, C. F. (1996). Transcending old age: creativity, development and psychoanalysis in the life of a centenarian. *International Journal of Psychoanalysis, 77*: 549–564.

Shakespeare, W. (1599). *As You Like It*. London: Edward Blount, and William and Isaac Jaggard, 1623.

Shapiro, B. (1999). Sibling rivalry: a phenomenon of construction and destruction. In: S. Akhtar & S. Kramer (Eds.), *Brothers and Sisters: Developmental, Dynamic, and Technical Aspects of the Sibling Relationship* (pp. 135–158). Northvale, NJ: Jason Aronson.

Shapiro, T. (1979). *Clinical Psycholinguistics*. New York: Plenum.

Sheehy, G. (1974). *Passages*. New York: Dutton.

Shneidman, E. (2008). *A Commonsense Book of Death*. Lanham, MD: Rowman & Littlefield.

Sievers, B. (2003). Your money or your life? Psychotic implications of the pension fund system: towards a socio-analysis of the financial services revolution. *Human Relations, 56*: 187–210.

Silberer, H. (1914). Problem der Mystik und ihrer Symbolik. Leipzig, Germany: Hugo Heller.

Singletary, W. (2001). Changing hateful feelings back to loving feelings: the work of child analysis. In: S. Akhtar (Ed.), *Three Faces of Mourning: Melancholia, Manic Defense, and Moving On* (pp. 141–156). Northvale, NJ: Jason Aronson.

Slater, M. H. (2015). Natural kindness. *British Journal for the Philosophy of Science, 66*: 375–411.

Smolen, A. (2006). An analysis with a latency age girl with post-traumatic stress disorder resulting in a secondary narcissistic personality disorder. *Journal of Infant, Child, and Adolescent Psychotherapy, 5*: 175–195.

Smolen, A. (2013). *Mothering Without a Home: Representations of Attachment Behaviors in Homeless Mothers and Children*. Lanham, MD: Jason Aronson.

Smolen, A. (2016). *Six Children: The Spectrum of Child Psychopathology and Its Treatment*. London: Karnac.

Solnit, A. (1983). The sibling experience. *Psychoanalytic Study of the Child, 38*: 281–284.

Spitz, R. (1946). The smiling response: a contribution to the ontogenesis of social relations. *Genetic Psychology Monographs, 34*: 57–125.

Spitz, R. (1953). Aggression: its role in the establishment of object relations. In: R. N. Emde (Ed.), *Rene A Spitz: Dialogues from Infancy* (pp. 321–331). New York: International Universities Press.

Spitz, R. (1960). Discussion of Dr John Bowlby's paper (Grief and mourning in infancy). *Psychoanalytic Study of the Child, 15*: 85–94.

Spitz, R. (1965). *The First Year of Life*. New York: International Universities Press.

Stein, M. (1985). Irony in psychoanalysis. *Journal of the American Psychoanalytic Association, 33*: 35–58.

Stern, D. B. (1985). *The Interpersonal World of the Infant: A View from Psychoanalysis and Developmental Psychology*. New York: Basic Books.

Stern, D. B. (1995). *The Motherhood Constellation: A Unified View of Parent–Infant Psychotherapy*. New York: Basic Books.

Stern, D. B. (2010). *Partners in Thought: Working with Unformulated Experience, Dissociation, and Enactment*. New York: Routledge.

Stern, D. N., Sander, L. W., Nahum, J. P., Harrison, A. M., Lyons-Ruth, K., Morgan, A. C., Bruschweiler-Stern, N., & Tronick, E. Z. (1998). Non-interpretative mechanisms in psychoanalytic therapy: the "something more" than interpretation. *International Journal of Psychoanalysis, 79*: 903–922.

Stoller, R. (1964). A contribution to the study of gender identity. *International Journal of Psychoanalysis, 45*: 220–226.

Stone, L. (1967). The psychoanalytic situation and transference—postscript to an earlier communication. *Journal of the American Psychoanalytic Association, 15*: 3–58.

Strachey, J. (1934). The nature of the therapeutic action of psychoanalysis. *International Journal of Psycho-Analysis, 50*: 275–292.

Sulloway, F. J. (1996). *Born to Rebel: Birth Order, Family Dynamics, and Creative Lives*. New York: Vintage.

Symington, N. (1981). The psychotherapy of a subnormal patient. *British Journal of Psychology, 54*: 167–199.

Tähkä, V. (1993). *Mind and Its Treatment: A Psychoanalytic Approach*. Madison, CT: International Universities Press.

Taketomo, Y. (1999). "Interpersonal amae" and "intrapsychic amae"—the problem of the psychoanalytic concept of amae as an extension of ordinary language amae. In: O. Kitayama (Ed.), *Clinical Practice in the Japanese Language, Volume III: Amae* (pp. 61–62). Tokyo: Seiwa Shoten.

Target, M., & Fonagy, P. (1996). Playing with reality, II: the development of psychic reality from a theoretical perspective. *International Journal of Psychoanalysis, 77*: 459–479.

Tausk, V. (1919). Über die Entstehung des "Beeinflussungsapparates" in der Schizophrenie. *International Journal of Psychoanalysis, 5*: 1–33.

Tessman, L. (1982). A note on the father's contribution to the daughter's way of loving and working. In: S. Cath, A. Gurwitt, & J. M. Ross (Eds.), *Father and Child* (pp. 219–238). Boston, MA: Little, Brown.

Thomas, A., & Chess, E. (1977). *Temperament and Development*. New York: Brunner/Mazel.

Tornstam, L. (2005). *A Developmental Theory of Positive Aging*. New York: Springer.

Tronick, E. Z. (1989). Emotions and emotional communication in infants. *American Psychologist, 44*: 112–119.

Tronick, E. Z. (2007). *The Neurobehavioral and Social-Emotional Development of Infants and Children*. New York: W. W. Norton.

Tummala-Narra, P. (2004). Mothering in a foreign land. *American Journal of Psychoanalysis, 64*: 167–181.

Tyson, P. (1988). Psychic structure formation: the complementary roles of affects, drives, object relations, and conflict. *Journal of the American Psychoanalytic Association, 36S*: 73–98.

Tyson, P. (2005). Separation-individuation, object constancy, and affect regulation. In: S. Akhtar & H. Blum (Eds.), *The Language of Emotions: Development, Psychopathology, and Technique* (pp. 69–82). Northvale, NJ: Jason Aronson.

U.S. Census Bureau (2018). *American Community Survey Reports.* Washington, DC: United States Congress, Census Bureau, pp. 1–25.

Vahip, I. (2017). Between diagnosis and death. In: S. Akhtar (Ed.), *Loss: Developmental, Cultural, and Clinical Realms* (pp. 194–205). London: Routledge.

Vaillant, G. (1977). *Adaptation to Life*. Boston, MA: Little, Brown.

Vallabhaneni, M. R. (2005). Advaita Vedanta, psychoanalysis, and the self. In: S. Akhtar (Ed.), *Freud Along the Ganges: Psychoanalytic Reflections on the People and Culture of India* (pp. 359–393). New York: Other Press.

Verheugt-Pleiter, A. J., Zevalkink, J., & Schmeets, M. G. (2008). *Mentalizing in Child Therapy*. London: Karnac.

Volkan, V. D. (1976). *Primitive Internalized Object Relations.* New York: International Universities Press.

Volkan, V. D., & Akhtar, S. (1997). *The Seed of Madness: Constitution, Environment, and Fantasy in the Organization of the Psychotic Core.* New York: International Universities Press.

Volkan, V. D., & Ast, G. (1997). *Siblings in the Unconscious and Psychopathology.* Madison, CT: International Universities Press.

Weil, A. (1970). The basic goal. *Psychoanalytic Study of the Child, 25*: 442–460.

Wheelis, A. (1966). *The Illusionless Man*. New York: Harper Colophon.

Wheelis, A. (1971). The league of death. In: *The Illusionless Man* (pp. 57–95). New York: Harper Colophon.

Wheelis, A. (1975). *On Not Knowing How to Live*. New York: Harper & Row.

Williams, M. (1972). Problems of technique during latency. *Psychoanalytic Study of the Child, 27*: 598–617.

Winnicott, D. W. (1945). Primitive emotional development. *International Journal of Psychoanalysis, 26*: 137–143.

Winnicott, D. W. (1946). Some psychological aspects of juvenile delinquency. In: C. Winnicott, R. Shepherd, & M. Davis (Eds.), *Deprivation and Delinquency* (pp. 113–119). London: Tavistock, 1984.

Winnicott, D. W. (1949). *The Ordinary Devoted Mother and Her Baby: Nine Broadcast Talks*. London: C. A. Brock.

Winnicott, D. W. (1952). Anxiety associated with insecurity. In: *Collected Papers: Through Paediatrics to Psychoanalysis* (pp. 97–100). New York: Basic Books, 1958.

Winnicott, D. W. (1953). Transitional objects and transitional phenomena. *International Journal of Psychoanalysis, 34*: 89–97.

Winnicott, D. W. (1954). The depressive position in normal emotional development. In: *Collected Papers: Through Paediatrics to Psychoanalysis* (pp. 262–277). London: Tavistock.

Winnicott, D. W. (1956a). Primary maternal preoccupation. In: *Collected Papers: Through Paediatrics to Psychoanalysis* (pp. 300–305). New York: Basic Books, 1958.

Winnicott, D. W. (1956b). The antisocial tendency. In: *Collected Papers: Through Paediatrics to Psychoanalysis* (pp. 306–316). New York: Basic Books, 1958.

Winnicott, D. W. (1960a). The theory of the parent–infant relationship. In: *The Maturational Processes and the Facilitating Environment* (pp. 37–55). New York: International Universities Press, 1965.

Winnicott, D. W. (1960b). Ego distortion in terms of true and false self. In: *The Maturational Processes and the Facilitating Environment* (pp. 140–152). New York: International Universities Press, 1965.

Winnicott, D. W. (1962). Ego integration in child development. In: *The Maturational Processes and the Facilitating Environment* (pp. 56–63). New York: International Universities Press.

Winnicott, D. W. (1963a). The development of the capacity for concern. In: *The Maturational Processes and the Facilitating Environment* (pp. 73–82). New York: International Universities Press, 1965.

Winnicott, D. W. (1963b). From dependence towards independence in the development of the individual. In: *The Maturational Processes and the Facilitating Environment* (pp. 83–92). New York: International Universities Press, 1965.

Winnicott, D. W. (1969). Breastfeeding as a communication. In: B. Brazelton, S. I. Greenspan, & B. Spock (Eds.), *Winnicott on the Child* (pp. 24–31). Cambridge, MA: Perseus, 2003.

Winzinger, M., Fallon, A., & Brabender, V. (2016). Mothers' experiences in creating an emotional connection with their adopted children: a qualitative analysis. In: S. Akhtar (Ed.), *The New Motherhoods: Patterns of Early Child Care in Contemporary Culture* (pp. 81–105). Lanham, MD: Rowman & Littlefield.

Wolf, E. (1994). Selfobject experiences: development, psychopathology, treatment. In: S. Kramer & S. Akhtar (Eds.), *Mahler and Kohut: Perspectives on Development, Psychopathology, and Technique* (pp. 65–96). Northvale, NJ: Jason Aronson.

Wolf, E. S. (1997). Selfobject experiences: Development, psychopathology, treatment. In: S. Kramer & S. Akhtar (Eds.), *Mahler and Kohut: Perspective on Development, Psychopathology, and Technique* (pp. 65–96). Northvale, NJ: Jason Aronson.

Wolman, T. (2017). Death of father. In: S. Akhtar & G. S. Kanwal (Eds.), *Bereavement: Personal Experiences and Clinical Reflections* (pp. 57–82). London: Karnac.

Wright, K. (1991). *Vision and Separation*. Northvale, NJ: Jason Aronson.

Zeligs, M. (1957). Acting in: a contribution to the meaning of some postural attitudes observed during analysis. *Journal of the American Psychoanalytic Association*, *5*: 685–706.

Index